UNCLE Yah Yah
21st Century Man of Wisdom
PART II

Al Dickens

UNCLE YAH YAH
21st Century Man of Wisdom

UNCLE YAH YAH
21st Century Man of Wisdom

Copyright © 2012 by Al Dickens. All rights reserved. The responsibility for the Theology expressed in this book is entirely that of the author, Al Dickens.

"Literature should not be suppressed merely because it offends the moral code of the censor."
-*Supreme Court Justice William* O. *Douglass* Dissent, Roth vs. U.S. 354 & U.S. 476-(1957)

Published by:
Yah Yah Publications
60 Evergreen Place Suite 904
East Orange, NJ 07018
www.yahyahpublications.com

An Imprint of·
Wahida Clark Presents Publishing
60 Evergreen Place Suite 904
East Orange, NJ 07018
973-678-9982
www.wclarkpublishing.com

ISBN 13 DIGIT 978-1-936649-01-3
ISBN 10 DIGIT 1-9366490-1-2
E-Book ISBN   978-1-936649-013

Library of Congress Control Number: 2011944440
Urban, Philosophy, Self-Help, Fiction, African American, Motivation, Fables, Spiritual, New Age.

UNCLE YAH YAH

21st Century Man of Wisdom

UNCLE YAH YAH

21st Century Man of Wisdom

Praise for Uncle Yah Yah 21st Century Man of Wisdom

Simplicity is the thing most easily delivered. "Uncle Yah Yah: 21st Century Man of Wisdom" is a collection of short stories from Al Dickens encouraging readers to embrace faith and improve their lives through these values. With no shortage of virtue within these pages, "Uncle Yah Yah" is a fun and inspiring read, highly recommended.
- The Midwest Book Review

Al Dickens's UNCLE YAH YAH is definitely one of those books that can inspire you and get you to thinking outside the box---whether it is fiction or not. The writer invites you to leave your comfort zone and analyze the way we see others and most importantly ourselves in relation to the world. The lessons are simply yet profound in that sometimes we have to be reminded of things that are right in front of our face. Definitely a book that was a long time in the works but well worth the wait and your time.
- C.A. Webb, *Conversations Book Club*

UNCLE YAH YAH
21st Century Man of Wisdom

Reading Uncle Yah Yah was one of the most inspiring things to ever happen to me. The smooth blend of illusion and reality made reading the book a sheer pleasure. The profound truth and insights contained in the book brought me face to face with my God consciousness and Divine purpose in life to serve God and humanity.
    -Dr. Henry. D. Muhammad Hamilton

My first intake on Uncle Yah Yah was that of excitement and anticipation. I just couldn't wait to get the manuscript. Uncle Yah Yah was very inspirational to me. It made me begin to teach and preach the sayings of Uncle Yah Yah.
    -Fred Pittman

It is a privilege to have received and read this little book that is a timely and timeless piece of literature. I liken these amazing pages to a contemporary societal Aesop's Fables. One cannot help but have his/her mind awakened to the simple yet profound truths causing us to question our collective human nature/psyche and the systems and beliefs we have built within our society.
    As a teacher, this book is a powerful tool for students to develop critical thinking skills by questioning and participating in dialogue with their peers. They can realize their integral place in

UNCLE YAH YAH
21st Century Man of Wisdom

society and how the choices they make will impact themselves and others for generations.

I applaud this book and its author. Mr. Dickens has great insight into the human condition and is able to communicate this wisdom with profound clarity.

-The Teacher

UNCLE YAH YAH
21st Century Man of Wisdom

UNCLE YAH YAH
21st Century Man of Wisdom

ACKNOWLEDGEMENTS

I wish to thank James Washington, Rubin "Hurricane" Carter, Tommy Trantino, Frank Earl Andrews, Nathan "Booby" Herd, Light Heavy Weight Contender James Scott, Melvin Van Peebles, Richard Widmark, and a host of others who inspired me to do this work.
-I truly thank you.

UNCLE YAH YAH
21st Century Man of Wisdom

UNCLE YAH YAH
21st Century Man of Wisdom

DEDICATION

To my father who used to say, "Boy, you ain't got a lick of sense." Thanks Pop, I needed that. To my wife, Wahida Clark Dickens, "I love you."

UNCLE YAH YAH

21st Century Man of Wisdom

UNCLE YAH YAH
21st Century Man of Wisdom

EDITOR'S NOTE

I found this book fascinating. It holds your interest and is very easy to read. Once you pick it up you can't put it down. But most importantly, it is the most thought-provoking book I've ever read.

The heart of this book is *Uncle Yah Yah's* manuscript, which is as Al explains it, the teachings of his spirit guide. Al shows a style all his own as his Aesopian-like fables unfold with the clarity and mystique of an ancient story teller. His exhortation that you learn about your society, understand what religion is and to know thy self are presented as a gift and not the dogmatic "Thou Shalt, or Thou Shalt Not." This

UNCLE YAH YAH
21st Century Man of Wisdom

is a learning experience you will not regret or forget.

Uncle Yah Yah is filled with common sense, but the importance of this book, I think, is that it gives another point of view. Its virtue lies in the fact that many of you will have to admit that you've never looked at the world from this angle before. It's timely and full of keys to turn the old rusty locks that bind and constrict us in our daily lives.

Come, let your mind travel through this crystal clear world with *Uncle Yah Yah, the 21st Century Man of Wisdom* and you will return from this voyage a richer person as I did.

-Wahida Clark New York Times and Essence Magazine Bestselling Author of: Thugs and The Women of Love Them, Every Thug Needs A Lady, Thug Matrimony, Thug Lovin', Payback is A Mutha, Payback With Ya Life, Sleeping With The Enemy, What's Really Hood? Vol. I, The Golden Hustla and Justify My Thug.

UNCLE YAH YAH
21st Century Man of Wisdom

FOREWORD

Read this book and you will agree that if there ever was any *One Who Flew Over the Cuckoo's Nest,* it had to be Al Dickens the author of this book. Sometimes truth is stranger than fiction. Even nature produces the uncommon or the unique at one time or another, like the duckbill platypus. So it is with this book; it is a genuine paradox.

It is strange, but true, that this book is filled with sane and sober truths that are presented in a most compassionate manner-though at times it may tug at the hemline of our old and ragged ideological garments and worn out customs. Yet, it is never offensive. After reading Uncle Yah Yah, you will agree it is a labor of love.

UNCLE YAH YAH
21st Century Man of Wisdom

It is strange, but true that the author is classified as a madman. Al Dickens is serving a sentence of fifty one years for bank robbery and has been confined for eleven years. Three years ago he was sent to the new Jersey State Hospital for the Criminally Insane. Since then he has been kept locked away in a cell in a special wing of the hospital designed for incorrigibles. The Vroom Building Readjustment Unit wing is the last stop of the New Jersey prison system and is called the "Snake Pit". No one comes out of there like they went in, if you can get out at all.

It is strange, but true, that this book, which is filled with wisdom and insight was written by a man who is psychologically diagnosed as a dangerous, paranoid schizophrenic and borderline mental-retard with an I.Q. of seventy-two. It is in this Snake Pit of wild adversity and zoo-like helplessness that Al Dickens wrote this book. It was his last hope to attempt to hold on to his sanity while most of those around him had long lost theirs.

Read and face the startling fact that this book *is strange, but true.* Read it and you will agree that sometimes the most profound ideas can come from the darkest dungeons of a crazy house.

UNCLE YAH YAH
21st Century Man of Wisdom

If Al Dickens is mad, then let us hope that every man can be affected by his brand of madness.

UNCLE YAH YAH

21st Century Man of Wisdom

UNCLE YAH YAH
21st Century Man of Wisdom

INTRODUCTION

I am *Uncle Yah Yah* and I have something to say to you. Whether the fools accept these small truths or not, I could care less. I must have my say.

Some of you will reject my words on first sight, without so much as a second glance. To you I say just one word: Fool! But to those of you who have the courage to at least sniff at my words before proclaiming that they stink, I offer you a little jewel of consummate wisdom.

It is to you courageous ones that I address these words. The weak hearted can't endure this fact-finding trip upon which we are about to embark.

The weak hearted are silly people, afraid of their own shadows. Whenever challenge raises his shaggy head, the poor cowards tremble and take flight, unaware that discover is the fruit of life; the fools dive headlong into the arms of the very death they think they are running from. Fear to learn new things is the worst kind of death.

But let us leave the weak hearted, chained to their fear and ignorance. We have no time to waste discussing the fools; in fact, the wisdom of a wise man can be measured according to the swiftness he displays in shunning the fools. So let's hurry into what matters. Read on.

-Uncle Yah Yah

UNCLE YAH YAH:

Twenty-First Century Man of Wisdom

Part II

By

Al Dickens

UNCLE YAH YAH: PART 2
21st Century Man of Wisdom

TRANSFORMATION
PART TWO

OUT OF CHAOS COMES congruity, so say Uncle Yah Yah. That's what he told me when I called him last week to ask his advice about my problems. I told him everything about my separation from my wife and children. Also, of my work being so hard I could hardly force myself to get out of bed in the mornings. I was so confused these days. I never thought that I, Rudy Hawkins, the star reporter, would be on the verge of a nervous breakdown.

I remember my wife yelling, "Rudy, you have lost your mind. Ever since you went to Paradise Gardens, you can't think about nothing, or talk about nothing but that old man Yah Yah. If you

UNCLE YAH YAH: PART 2
21st Century Man of Wisdom

want to give up all that we have worked for and go up there and live in the woods with that old man, then you go ahead. But you can forget about me and the children because we are leaving."

I didn't believe she would really leave, but she packed her and the children some things and went to my mother's house. Two weeks have passed. I am alone. I haven't been to work in three days. This house looks like a junkyard.

That's when I decided to call Uncle Yah Yah. He listened to all I had to say, and then said, "Good, good. Everything is fine. You are coming into your own. Soon, you will know who you are and your work in this life. Remember, after difficulty comes ease, and out of chaos comes congruity. Then he said, "See you when you get here, and hurry up."

Two days later, I was still as confused as ever. I had been away from work for five days. I decided to call the office.

"Hello, Essex Weekly News," Jonathan's voice came over the line.

"Hey Boss, I'm just calling to let you know that I'm still living. How's Carol?"

"Rudy, my man. How you doing, stranger? And when in the world are you coming back to work?"

"That's what I'm calling about. I'm going to take my two week's vacation. Can you manage without me?"

Jonathan was quiet for a few seconds, and then he said, "Sure, when do you want to go, or have you already started?" He laughed.

"Yeah, right. I'm leaving today. Tell Carol and Dottie I'll see them in two weeks."

"Dottie doesn't work here anymore. She left and went up to Paradise Garden to live and work near Uncle Yah Yah. I thought you knew that," Jonathan said.

"What! Dottie went up to Cuddybackville to stay?" I was shocked.

"Yeah. She said it was something she had to do. So we gave her a going away party right here in the office three days ago."

"Well, ain't that something. I missed out."

"Where are you going, Rudy?"

"I'm going to go and spend a little time with Uncle Yah Yah."

"What! Wait a minute. This is too much. You mean to say you are going up there, too?"

UNCLE YAH YAH: PART 2
21st Century Man of Wisdom

BACK IN HEAVEN

PARADISE GARDENS HAD NOT changed much from the last time I was there, aside from the exceptional high I noticed as soon as I parked my car in front of the main office. It was a very calm feeling, a feeling of peace. I wasn't tense anymore. I just felt good.

In the registration office I said my hellos to Sue the receptionist and her mother, Mrs. Sally Walters. They said they were glad to see me and even happier to hear that this time I was there on vacation.

After a little chat about how everyone was doing, I made my way to cabin seven. This was the same cabin I had the last time I was here. I saw that as a good omen.

While I was in the parking lot taking my

UNCLE YAH YAH: PART 2
21st Century Man of Wisdom

bags out of the trunk, I noticed some people engaged in some busy activity in front of the big red barn. I recalled a party I went to in that barn the last time I was here. The inside had been converted into a dance hall. I wondered what was going on down there. I was soon to find out.

The first person to visit my cabin was Sue's husband, Brother-in-law Dear. He stuck his head through the open door and yelled, "What's happening, my man?" He came in and gave me a big hug. "We heard you were coming and everybody's expecting you."

"Brother-in-law Dear, it is good to see you. How are you doing? What's been going on up here since I've been gone?" I inquired as I offered him a chair. "Tell me about Uncle Yah Yah and Aunt Willie Mae. Are they all right? And Freda, how is she?"

"Everyone is doing fine. I just left Uncle Yah Yah's house. They are all happy you are back. Listen Rudy, I can't stay right now. I just stopped by to welcome you back. I was on my way down to the barn to help put the finishing touches on for the party tonight."

"A party?" I asked.

"Yeah. It's for Uncle Yah Yah. He just came down from his cabin retreat in the

UNCLE YAH YAH: PART 2
21st Century Man of Wisdom

mountain. He was up there fasting and praying for forty days and forty nights. And now it's party time. All the family will be there. A lot of our friends and some of Uncle Yah Yah's closest companions will also be there. You got here at the right time."

"Will Freda be there?" I asked.

"Oh yeah, Freda said she will see you at the party tonight. Uncle Yah Yah said to bring your tape recorder." Brother-in-law Dear started for the door as he said, "I'll see you tonight."

He was almost out the door when I blurted out, "What time will it start?"

"Seven. So be there," he said.

"One more thing, Brother-in-law. Did a young woman named Dottie Schleifa register here a few days ago?"

"Yeah. She told us you planned to come back up here. She will be there tonight too. Now I really have to go. See you at the party tonight," he said as he closed the door and was gone.

I looked at my watch; I had a little more than an hour to get ready. I had to shower and shave. I was very excited about the way things were turning out. I couldn't wait to see Freda, Dottie, and especially Uncle Yah Yah.

UNCLE YAH YAH: PART 2
21st Century Man of Wisdom

THE PARTY

IT WAS SEVEN O'CLOCK WHEN I started to leave the cabin. As I closed the door I remembered the tape recorder. I went back to get it and put a 90 minute blank tape in it. I then locked the door and headed for the party.

The grounds were lit up with colorful party lights. People were standing around and a sense of gaiety filled the air. Japanese lanterns lit the path to the barn. It was a wonderful sight and a good feeling came over me.

I stepped through the barn door and was confronted with another beautiful sight. Party decorations were all over the place. Around the perimeter of the dance floor were tables covered with red and white checkerboard tablecloths with bowls of fresh fruit on top. Right in front of the bandstand was a long

UNCLE YAH YAH: PART 2
21st Century Man of Wisdom

table with a white tablecloth and several bowls of fruit and pitchers of ice water on it.

"Rudy!"

Startled out of my thoughts, I looked around and there she was.

"Freda! How you doing?" I said as I gave her a big hug and a kiss.

"I've got you now, Rudy. It's about time you found the way back here," she teased. "Ain't you going to speak to Dottie?" she said, pointing to my right.

I looked and sure enough it was Dottie. "You ran off and didn't tell me you were coming here," I said as I grabbed and hugged her.

"I would have told you had I seen you, but you left the job and didn't even show up for my going away party," she said, returning my hug.

"Yeah, well, we are all here now and I'm happy about the way this whole thing has turned out."

Suddenly, people were standing and clapping their hands.

"What's going on?" I asked Freda.

"Uncle Yah Yah is here." She pointed toward the bandstand. The clapping grew even louder. We could hardly hear ourselves talk.

UNCLE YAH YAH: PART 2
21st Century Man of Wisdom

"We are getting ready to start," Freda said.

I looked at the table where Uncle Yah Yah was standing, and I saw some men, all dressed alike in dark suits and a few women dressed in white gowns.

"Who are the people at the table with Uncle Yah Yah?" I asked.

"They are his chief companions and disciples. They will sit at the table with him. You will be at the table with him also. He wants you to record the question and answer session," Freda told me.

"Where will you and Dottie be?"

"Right over there at the little table, the second one from the front. We'll be waiting for you."

"Okay," I said, "I'll be right there as soon as I can get away."

"Will everyone please be seated!" came the pleasant voice of one of the dark suited men, who had the microphone in his hand. I left Freda and Dottie and went to the long table. It reminded me of the biblical scene The Last Supper.

Uncle Yah Yah saw me and waved for me to come around to his side of the table. He greeted me as if I had been there all the time. Then Uncle Yah Yah said, "Okay Rudy, get one of those chairs over there and bring it right here behind my chair. I want you close, so you can record everything during the question and answer period."

I did as I was told, and as soon as I was in position with the recorder ready, the man in the dark suit began to speak.

"Is everybody peaceful?"

"Yes we are," responded the crowd. The emcee continued.

"Are we going to party tonight?"

"Yes we are," answered the crowd.

"Are we happy to have our beloved Uncle Yah Yah back with us tonight?"

"Yes we are," resounded the response of those present.

"Well then, without any further delay, I now present to you the Master Teacher of us all, Uncle Yah Yah!"

The crowd was on their feet clapping their hands gaily. Uncle Yah Yah stood and raised his hands to quiet the crowd. In less than three seconds the crowd was seated and so quiet you could hear your own heart beat.

"May God bless you all for coming out to be with your teacher tonight. May God's peace be with us all, and may we have a good time tonight," Uncle Yah Yah said as he gazed around the hall with a broad smile.

"I had a very successful fast. It lasted for forty days and forty nights. I did some writing, some praying, and a lot of thinking about food."

The crowd burst into laughter and I was reminded of the fun way Uncle Yah Yah expressed himself.

When the crowd was quiet again, Uncle Yah Yah said, "We will start the festivities as we always do and that is with questions and answers. But the questions must come from the host at this table. That is our tradition. So let's start with the questions, so we can get this session out of the way. I'm hungry enough to eat my shoes."

Uncle Yah Yah sat down and said, "Okay, let's have the first question."

A woman in a white gown raised her hand and asked, "Uncle Yah Yah, is marriage on the decline and what will be the consequences if it is?"

UNCLE YAH YAH: PART 2
21st Century Man of Wisdom

MARRIAGE ON THE DECLINE

THE INSTITUTION OF MARRIAGE is deteriorating throughout the so-called civilized world. Man discovered a long time ago that the freedom to express his sexual urge whenever, and with whomever, was like turning wild horses loose in the dining room.

If civilization was to succeed, a bridle had to be put on that wild animal called sex. Man reasoned that sex-control was self-control, and a controlled society is a progressive society.

Marriage was one of the first educational institutions. The civilization that controlled mating, through marriage, is the one that reaches the highest standards of greatness and productivity, as well as population growth.

Man thought marriage was purely for

reproduction. Free love was considered savage. Man fashioned marriage to be the great civilizer.

Once married, he must be dutiful to raising and caring for his family. He had to be brave as the protector of his home. He became a great thinker in his attempt to provide love and comfort.

It is love and all its expressions, as a result of personal attraction, that has made the greatest contributions to the world today. Making love makes one lovable and that love expresses itself in all we do.

Two foolish and egotistical people cannot establish a lasting and successful marriage. Ignorant people cannot educate children and be self-sacrificing, compromising, and dedicated. Marriage is supposed to bring out the best in man.

One of the leading indicators that a civilization is on the decline is the breakdown of its control of sex. Large numbers of unmarried people, and the general acceptance of free sex, is a true sign that society as we know it is declining.

Some other reasons for this type of decay is the change brought about by modern societies' commitment to industry and not to the promotion of family ties and values. Many years before the technological revolution took place, family was important.

Family was stabilized by property, finance, and affluence. The bigger the family, the better. Marriage was a life-long commitment. The husband and wife had a mission of welding the family together and educating them to survive as a unit. Family 'comes first' was their maxim. Also, women today are fast becoming independent in the workplace, and are demanding more of an individual choice in marriage, having and rearing children, and their careers.

The public schools have taken over the raising of the children, and are preparing them for industry and not for raising their own future families. If family values are not taught at home, the children of the twenty-first century will have no idea about family or care for a family.

Therefore, I say marriage as we have known it is dead. It has out-lived its usefulness in today's society.

Consequently, I believe, there will soon be no long-term commitments called marriage. People will live together on whim and fancy. Sex will become purely recreational, because males and females will be government protected from having children.

The government will make all citizens sterile with a shot in the arm, which will only be reversed by a government license and at a high cost.

Government will take childbearing and child rearing from the private citizen. Yes, Big Brother will decide which male sperm goes into the sperm bank and which female ova. They will decide how many test-tube babies there will be, and how many surrogate mothers will be implanted for natural birth per year. The ultimate birth control. I see sexually transmitted diseases being wiped out within ten years. Sexual love, commitment, and responsibility will be called old fashioned. Sex will be as free as asking for a cigarette or a drink of water.

Can you imagine waiting at a bus stop and being asked by a total stranger for some sex? You check your watch and answer according to the bus schedule.

"Yes, but it's got to be a quickie. I've got ten minutes."

Marriage as we have known it is dead, and is now stinking in the nostrils of God. Did you know that the aboriginal tribe called African

UNCLE YAH YAH: PART 2
21st Century Man of Wisdom

Pygmies have no marital institution? But that's another story.

UNCLE YAH YAH: PART 2
21st Century Man of Wisdom

MARIJUANA

A DARK SUITED MAN SITTING two seats to the right of Yah Yah asked him, "What about smoking marijuana, and will it ever be legalized?"

History repeats itself. What goes around, comes around. Marijuana smoking is as old as recorded history.

The same thing that is happening now with reefer was happening with alcohol during the prohibition days from 1920 to 1933. Back then, Federal agents were out busting folks for making and selling whiskey—moonshine, they called it.

Today, agents are arresting growers and sellers of marijuana. But just like it was back then with so many people drinking, the government had to legalize alcohol. Billions of dollars now go to the government from the tax

UNCLE YAH YAH: PART 2
21st Century Man of Wisdom

on alcohol.

A few days ago, government approved the sale of marijuana in drug stores. So it won't be long before it will be decriminalized and then legalized.

There are about 44 billion dollars spent on reefer each year. That represents a lot of tax dollars the government is missing out on. A lot can be done with the tax dollars from the sale of reefer. We have five hundred thousand heroin addicts in this country. If marijuana was taxed and legalized, it would support the best treatment and rehabilitation programs money could buy.

The government has been hell bent on preaching the evils of smoking marijuana while completely ignoring the hundreds of good uses the reefer plant has provided for thousands of years.

Today's doctors are learning that the ancient people knew what they were doing when using marijuana for healing the sick. Doctors are now treating leukemia and stomach cancer with reefer.

I am told that people using valium are better off smoking reefer because valium causes memory lost and cannabis doesn't. Yet, reefer relaxes and calms the user.

UNCLE YAH YAH: PART 2
21st Century Man of Wisdom

The first report in English literature on the marijuana plant and its medical use was done by a British army physician, Dr. Sir William O'Shaughnessy, 1838.

Marijuana is not just a physical healer. The great euphoric state of consciousness produced as a result of ingesting reefer is universally known. It stimulates the imaginative.

Some say it puts you in touch with God. I guess that's one of the reasons why many of the Eastern and African religions are rooted in marijuana smoking. Here in the western hemisphere the Rastafarians are in a court battle because reefer is illegal. They are being denied the First Amendment Right, religious freedom. Smoking reefer is a sacred rite in many religions.

Did you know that marijuana was one of the most important crops during the Colonial Era? And that George Washington, Thomas Jefferson, and Ben Franklin all grew marijuana? Well, they did! All of them had farms and plantations.

Hemp was of great commercial use. Hemp rope and cloth were in big demand. Reefer is one of the oldest and most versatile plants on this planet. It was brought and sold freely until 1937; this was when the Federal Bureau of

UNCLE YAH YAH: PART 2
21st Century Man of Wisdom

Narcotics pushed congress to pass the Marijuana Tax Act. And to this very day the government doesn't separate marijuana from heroin and cocaine.

Black slaves worked those reefer plantations and knew very well of the many ways to use it and smoke it. The use of marijuana by the slaves in colonial times was a closely guarded secret. If the slave master caught them in the act of using it, they would tell him, "We are just burning some roots and worshipping God." Many of the slaves came from central and West Africa where the tradition of reefer-smoking-religious-cults dated back hundreds of years. These Africans brought the practice of smoking reefer to the New World.

White folks would say, "Why is them niggers always grinning, singing, and dancing? Ain't they tired from working in them fields?" Could this have been attributed to reefer? Maybe not in every case, but nonetheless, if you put a rabbit in a carrot patch, the only way that rabbit won't have himself a feast is if he doesn't know what he is working with.

Those early Africans knew what marijuana was and how to use it, as well as hundreds of other plants and herbs.

UNCLE YAH YAH: PART 2
21st Century Man of Wisdom

"Yes," Uncle Yah Yah said, "I think it will be legalized soon. My opinion is that smoking marijuana is such a little sin, but such a big blessing."

UNCLE YAH YAH: PART 2
21st Century Man of Wisdom

GOD AND THE DEVIL

ANOTHER LADY IN A WHITE GOWN raised her hand and asked, "Uncle Yah, is God dead?"

"No, God is not dead! He is more alive now than ever before. But religion is dead! That old idea of God being somewhere in the sky, eating dates, and listening to jazz being played by angels with harps made of gold, has been reduced to the status of old wives tales.

"Even the foolish twenty-first century man is seeing through the 'prayer for dollars' church of God. Since when do we have to pay God for the forgiveness of our sins?

"Church members are being asked to leave the congregation if they fail to keep up their donations. If God is your Lord, why does he need someone to talk to Him for your sake?

"God is in you, controlling your life. No

UNCLE YAH YAH: PART 2
21st Century Man of Wisdom

one can speak to God for you. That reminds me of the story about the devil and the preachers.

"They were having a big party at the governor's mansion. Satan was one of the honored guests. He was dancing, drinking, and having a ball. Suddenly, Gabriel, the Sword of God showed up. The devil panicked. He ran and jumped into his red Corvette and sped off down the highway.

"Just as he began to feel safe from Gabriel, a plane shot out of the clear blue sky like a bolt of lightning. Old Gabe was piloting a jet-propelled helicopter; it was a warship that looked like a baby B-1 bomber. Gabriel fired two hawk missiles that exploded right in the path of the devil's car. Satan swerved, hit the embankment, and the car turned over and burst into flames.

"Gabriel flew off into the blue eastern sky believing his mission was complete. But Satan, that old crafty devil, was not through yet. Severely injured, but not dead, he lay there in his burning Corvette.

"A poor man, who was a little drunk, was the first to arrive at the crash site. The flames were almost extinguished. The drunk bent over to look inside the car. Instantly, the devil

UNCLE YAH YAH: PART 2
21st Century Man of Wisdom

reached out and grabbed his wrist and said, 'I am the devil! Help me out of this and I'll give you all the whiskey in the world.' Just as the devil was convincing the drunk of his authenticity, a white Rolls Royce pulled up to the accident. A minister, a priest and a rabbi got out and rushed over to help.

"The drunk pulled himself free of the devil's grip and ran shouting toward the clergymen, 'Stop, stop! The devil is in that car. He is wounded, but he ain't dead yet. Give me some gasoline, so I can finish him off for good.'

"The minister said, 'This man is drunk.'

"The priest said, 'Do you have any proof of that?'

"The drunk said, 'Here is his wallet with a driver's license and some credit cards. He told me he would make me rich, famous and he would give me all the whiskey in the world, if I'd help him out.'

"The rabbi, checking out the wallet, said, 'Yeah, its Lucifer all right. Here is an identification picture. So what are we going to do now?'

"Old wicked Lucifer seized upon the moment. Taking advantage of their indecision, he said, 'You had better get your fat butts over here and get me to a hospital, and be quick about it.'

"The clergy said as one, 'Why should we do that?'

"Satan said, 'Because we are partners, and if I die there will be no more sin in the world. If there is no sin, there will be no need for the Church. No Church, no big homes, big cars, or big money. Do you know what I mean?'

"The clergy all said together, 'Right!'

"They pushed the poor drunk aside, pulled old Lucifer from the wreck, and was last seen speeding south along the highway in the direction of the Medical Burn Center.

"You may laugh at my little absurd story, but think of how foolish we are in believing such trash as God is a spook that you can't see until you die, and that He lives somewhere in the sky, and that the only ones who know Him and talk to Him are the preachers.

"They have special words, some mumbo jumbo that they keep secret from us. Whenever we need God, we have to come first to these self-proclaimed God brokers. For a fee they will contact Him for us. Bull shoes! We are not that dumb anymore. Even a dumb dog can tell the difference between being stumbled over and being intentionally kicked.

UNCLE YAH YAH: PART 2
21st Century Man of Wisdom

People are now waking up to the real deal.

"Your body is the true Temple of God. This is the great secret they kept from us for so long. If you knew that God was in you, and is you, then you wouldn't need a church nor a preacher to pay and ask to pray for you. The Church is the richest institution on the planet today!

"We are all gods. We come from a god-state and we are now returning to Godhood. We need nothing, or no one, but the One True and living God.

"He Lives!"

UNCLE YAH YAH: PART 2
21st Century Man of Wisdom

WAR

ANOTHER MAN IN A DARK SUIT raised his hand and asked, "Do you think we will have a third world war?"

Uncle Yah Yah took his time to answer that question. He took a sip of water and looked around at his audience. It was so quiet you could hear the crickets talking to each other.

Uncle Yah Yah broke the silence by saying, "That is a very good question, and I'm glad it came up tonight because this is a timely issue.

"War is not coming; it is already here! War is necessary and desirable at this time. If Mr. Reagan can find a neat little country to declare war against, like Nicaragua, he and Mr. Bush, could stay in the White House because all elections are suspended during the time of

UNCLE YAH YAH: PART 2
21st Century Man of Wisdom

war.

"Also, because of the capitalist system we live in, makes it necessary to fight a major war every 25 to 30 years. Capitalism allows private enterprise to flood the markets with their products. In about 25 years, the markets are saturated. An example in point is the portable radio. Once everyone has a radio, the market slows down to just a few sales. The manufacturer lays off his workers, and in a lot of cases, closes down production.

"The masses become hungry and dissatisfied. Civil disorder breaks out throughout the country. Anarchy steps in and the government will fail, unless something happens that will bring all the people together again.

"You guessed right, war! That is what will bring the radio industry back; working 24-hours non-stop under government contract, making military radios and communications equipment for the armed forces.

"The clothing industry will be making uniforms and parachutes. The shoe industry will be making boots. In fact, all industries will have a new market, working for the war effort.

"Ship builders will go back to work and the

UNCLE YAH YAH: PART 2
21st Century Man of Wisdom

steel mills will reopen. The automotive industry will make trucks, tanks, and jeeps. Everybody will have plenty of work. The people become united because they all have family and friends fighting in the war.

"No, it will not be a nuclear war. They, the superpowers, have decided not to use nuclear weapons. They will fight a conventional war like they did in Vietnam and in World War II. They know there is no winner in a nuclear war.

"Another funny reason they won't use the big bomb is because their scientist have concluded the only people most likely to survive a nuclear war are those with melanin. This is dark pigment in the body of black people! So, believe me, white folks are not going to blow themselves off this good planet and leave it all to us. They will use a little gas and every other tactic they can use against each other. America and her allies will destroy Russia, England, France, West Germany, and the other European friends will kick down the Soviet's front door.

"China and the Eastern allies will break through Russia's back door. It will be over almost before it begins. But the allies will argue over the spoils of war. Some will leave

UNCLE YAH YAH: PART 2
21st Century Man of Wisdom

the alliance and some will threaten to leave; there will be much confusion.

"America, fearing the continued loss of helping nations, contrives to attack Communist China. Attacking China before she becomes industrially and technologically too big to handle, America will reason, this will allow her to keep what few allies are left because they will not leave America to fight it out with China alone. That will prove to be a big mistake for America. China will whistle America to her knees, and with the threat of being totally over-run, America will use her nuclear power to stop the Chinese invasion. China will be destroyed, but America's back will be broken. Never again will she regain her posture as the world's leading Super Power.

"Yes, the war is already going on. A sharp eye and a little sense will let you see it. For example, every time this government goes to war, it enlists an over abundant amount of Blacks and Hispanics into the military. Hey, that's just the way it is. Another sign is the prisons. There are 650,000 men and women in the Nation's prisons. People stacked up, and in some cases they are sleeping on floors. There are not enough jails to hold them all, and there are still more coming into the system every

UNCLE YAH YAH: PART 2
21st Century Man of Wisdom

day. About 89% of the prisoners are Black and Hispanic.

"As of this date, there are six states with government programs to train prison inmates to enter the military. This program trains and inducts inmates directly into the armed forces and expunges their criminal records. They train for 90 days and off they go. Why else would they stuff the jails if getting ready to fight this war wasn't the real plan in the first place?

"I see it happening like this—Nicaragua attacks the Contras. The President declares war on Nicaragua. Cuba comes to the aid of President Ortega of Nicaragua, and America invades Cuba. Russia comes to the aid of Cuba and attacks West Germany. The Allies counterattack Russia. And the rest is history.

"However, all is not lost. There are some good things that come out of war. Money is in abundance during wartime. It is said that even the ragman gets rich during the time of war. At the conclusion of the war, many people who were poor and penniless will be wealthy. They will make up a whole new class of New Rich.

"But that's another story."

UNCLE YAH YAH: PART 2
21st Century Man of Wisdom

ONENESS WITH GOD

EVERYONE IN THE PLACE appeared to be in deep thought. If all these people came to get something to think about, well, they were sure getting it.

My mind was racing. I looked at Uncle Yah Yah. He looked fresh, like he was just warming up and was ready to answer questions all night if need be.

Another arm was raised and the question asked was, "How do you become one with God?"

"That's another good question," Uncle Yah Yah said.

"There is an old saying that if you prepare a meal for a man, that man eats for one day. But if you teach him to prepare a meal for himself, then he will eat for the rest of his life. Only the divinely blessed, the pure of heart, can accept and practice this knowledge that brings you face to face with God. Once you have it, you are duty bound to pass it on to your fellow man.

"Any rich man can feed the poor, but only a disciple of God can feed the soul of man with the bread of Truth. Repeat the message with every chance you get, until every man, woman, and child are the servants of God.

"God's will is for man to become perfect and live forever in peace and happiness. Therefore, man must learn wisdom in order to understand life's true value and to know what is real and what is unreal. Money and domination of your fellow man is short-lived, and can't stand the test of time, so they are unreal. The attributes of God are everlasting and are reality.

"There is no greater knowledge than the knowledge of God, and His purpose for the future of man. There is no greater glory than to be an agent of God, working to bring about the universal evolution of man. That is the truly beautiful life. Doing God's work gives you the greatest pleasure.

"As God's helper, we must learn to do the right thing at the right time. Desire nothing but to be like, or as, God. Surely, what you worship you do become. You must see God in everyone and everything. Only speak the truth. Be fearless of all besides God.

"You must win the battle of self-control, and let nothing take you off your path. Be peaceful. What you do today prepares your tomorrow. Trust God only. Help those who want help. Teach those that want to be taught. Mind your own business. Never gossip. Know that only God is great.

"These are godly qualities, and when you practice them you are God, and you will want only what God wills. It is a great learning experience and can only be achieved through your faith in God the Almighty.

"To control yourself you must know yourself. You must learn the different levels of the mind and their functions. Once you can identify the parts of your mind, you will be able to stay in touch with the real you. The real you is the soul; that is the throne of God.

"Each part of the mind tries to impose itself on you to do its will, but you must recognize their tricks and make them obey the real you. God.

"The conscious mind deals with the rational world and the intellect. The subconscious is the storehouse of the memory, the channel for the clairvoyant and the clairaudient; it's the vehicle for inspiration and genius. The subconscious is a powerful instrument to bring you face to face with God. But you don't worship the vehicle that brings you to God's house, you worship and obey God.

"A wise friend of mine by the name of Alcyone wrote very positive instruction in the book At the Feet of the Master. It says, 'You must dig deep down into yourself to find the God within you, and listen to His voice, which is your voice. Do not mistake your body for yourself—neither the physical body, nor astral, nor the mental. Each one of them will pretend to be the Self, in order to gain what it wants, but you must know them all, and know yourself as their master.'

"He further says, 'The astral body has its desires, dozens of them; it wants you to be angry, to say sharp words, to feel jealous, to be greedy for money, to envy other people their possessions, and to yield yourself to depression. All these things it wants, and many more, not because it wishes to harm you, but because it likes violent vibrations and likes to change them constantly. You must discriminate between your wants and your body's.'

And he continues with, 'Your mental body wishes to think itself proudly separate, to think much of itself and little of others, and even when you have turned it away from worldly things, it still tries to calculate for self, to make you think of your own progress instead of thinking of the Master's work and of helping others. When you meditate, it will try to make you think of the many different things which it wants instead of the one thing which you want. You are not this mind, but it is yours to use, so here again, discrimination is necessary. You must watch unceasingly, or you will fail."

So Uncle Yah Yah continued, "It is up to every one of us to discipline ourselves, learn God's ways, and His will. Then, we must teach it to others. The Bible says, 'Ye are all gods and children of the Most High.'"

UNCLE YAH YAH: PART 2
21st Century Man of Wisdom

FOOD

"UNCLE YAH YAH, I DON'T WANT to sound crazy, but this question has been on my mind for some time now," one of the men sitting across from Uncle Yah Yah said.

But before he could finish, Uncle Yah Yah said, "Paul said 'Prove all things and that which you find true, hold on to it.' And I would like to add to that by saying, ask questions and you will learn all about yourself.

"So what is your question?" asked Uncle Yah Yah.

"Is it true that there was a time when man did not eat food?"

"Yes, that was trillions of years ago. At one time the Earth was known as the Blue Planet, the Home of the Gods. We were in an orbit much closer to the sun than we are now. The

UNCLE YAH YAH: PART 2
21st Century Man of Wisdom

Blue Planet was approximately thirty-five thousand miles in circumference, and we used Mars and Venus as our satellites. "But a bad situation was brought about, having a Star Wars and a Darth Vader effect on the Blue Planet. A dissatisfied member of the Royal Family tried to take over. Failing in his attempt to overthrow the Kingdom, he ignited a nuclear doomsday explosion, expecting to destroy the planet. "The bomb fell short of its mark and resulted in blowing off a big chunk of the Blue Planet. That piece is our present day moon. The planet was thrown out of its original orbit around the sun. It, the earth, fell with the moon piece, following it until it was caught in its present magnetic field, and began a new orbit with its new moon.

"The Royal Family, being forewarned, was able to take the family, along with many of the citizens and other life forms, into a large spaceship. They escaped to safety to await the settling of the water and the atmosphere, which were affected by the explosion. They then came to earth and established civilization. They knew that the discovery of the evil forces or devil would continue to repeat itself, unless the Royal Family allowed for its total manifestation. So the wise fathers decided to

UNCLE YAH YAH: PART 2
21st Century Man of Wisdom

give this evil a place in time to dominate the supreme beings. But this would mean the sacrifice of power to live indefinitely, of being disease free, and the lost of psychic powers.

"They knew that superior wisdom could not be subjected to weakness, so in order for the dark side to have freedom of expression, eating food was instituted.

"All food is poisonous. The more you eat, the faster you die. Before eating became the rule, we needed only to breathe and take in the nourishment from the air.

"At first, we ate only when we were ready to die. We would have a big party, eat a lot of different foods and the poison would kill us. Our systems were so clean they couldn't fight off the accumulation of poison consumed at a fast rate.

"As we continued to eat, our systems got used to it, but we caught diseases and died. The quality of life we had disappeared. People started eating to show that they were affluent. If you could afford to throw a party, you were rich. Then eating became commonplace, and sickness and death were just facts of life.

"The Supreme Father allowed all of this in order to know and control the dark side. Life and death, heaven and hell.

UNCLE YAH YAH: PART 2
21st Century Man of Wisdom

"The less you eat, the longer you live, and the better the quality of your life. The plan is to reverse the levers, so to say, on eating in the last days of spiritual darkness. People will stop eating and killing themselves. Health and the great powers they had in the beginning will be theirs in the end of the dark days.

"Eating kills, fasting preserves and prolongs life. Food of the gods is whole wheat bread, fruit and milk."

UNCLE YAH YAH: PART 2
21st Century Man of Wisdom

GOOD SEX

"I THINK IT'S TIME TO GIVE UNCLE Yah Yah a break," the man acting as emcee said. But Uncle Yah Yah interrupted him.

"I'll take a few more. I'm enjoying myself. These have been some very beautiful questions."

The crowd began clapping in approval. They wanted to hear more.

The next question came from the end of the long table. The woman asked, "What is good sex?"

"Sexuality in this country is a major problem. This is due to lack of proper education. Sex wise, America is on the bottom level, like kindergarten is to college."

"Scientists have proven that sex must be

taught; it is not instinctive. You don't grow up knowing what to do. But due to religious restrictions, and the belief that all sex was sinful and evil, not only was it not taught as it should have been, but people, to this very day, are afraid to even talk about it.

"Ask any experienced prostitute and she will tell you that the majority of her clients don't know how to have sex. Most men blame their wives for their seeking out prostitutes. They say they can't satisfy their wives because their wives have problems. The fact is, it is the men with the problems. According to prostitutes, some men will take off their clothes, jump on top of them, make a few feeble motions, and are finished in less than three minutes most of the time. Then they think they are red-hot lovers.

"It is ignorance to think this problem will go away by itself if we just don't talk about it. How can we look the other way when divorce rates are continually sky rocketing? Sex related crimes are on the increase, along with mental illness, as a direct result of sexual inadequacies, and crowding people in prisons and crazy houses.

"We must begin to teach everything modern society knows about sex, the good and the bad, and how to have or share sex. It is a shame that we have grown men and women who have been married twenty and thirty years, and still don't know each other's sexual preferences. Some have never looked at, or even touched, the other's genitals. They still have sex in the dark and never talk about it. We must kill the idea that sex is dirty.

"Every school should have a library of all the exotic literature of every nation on earth. Students should be taught how to discover their own sexual preferences, and how to communicate those sexual desires to their mates.

"It is the pitiful lack of knowledge which permits the publishing of college level biology books, which show pictures of human beings without vaginas and penises. We must take sex out of the dark ages. We must teach the true and scientific enlightenment of sex in this twenty-first century. It is too important to our mental and physical existence to ignore. Our mental and physical well-being depends on our ability to experience good sex.

"The physical expression of sex is for reproduction and pleasure. It's the greatest physical pleasure experienced by man. The mutual gratification brought about by proper

UNCLE YAH YAH: PART 2
21st Century Man of Wisdom

communication with your mate is strengthening and healthy. "But there is a greater function to sex, it is the spiritual side. Sex is the highest expression of man and woman; it is on this level that their communication can be the purest. The highest spiritual communication is prayer to God.

"I don't expect all of you to understand this concept. The wise will pick up on it. So I'll just state a few facts about Holy sexual union and drop this subject.

"Holy sexual union is so great it will give you a power that will make an atom bomb look like a cap pistol. However, if you don't know who you are you can't choose a proper mate. Without the proper mate you will get nowhere with Holy sexual union. If you don't know self you can't recognize your mate.

"Everything is created in pairs. Love is organic and chemical unity. Blood is the spirit, unity of blood is unity of spirit. When you and your mate are as one in sexual union, you create a force stronger than the material world. Being in tune physically and spiritually, they create the temple of God, and the uniting of the positive and negative forces of the universe. In this sacred, divine, and holy atmosphere, they become one with God in the pure state of existence. The goals and dreams which they hold onto with both their hearts, and strongly desire, they will create the power to call together the material world and fashion its likeness into reality.

"The man recites and the woman repeats his words. He says, 'O Great Lord of all that is and all that will ever be. Grant us, your servants, an orphanage, that we may be the nursing mothers and fathers to these homeless children, and we shall teach them Thy praise.'

"Needless to say, this above science has been kept secret from the masses because it destroys the need for religion, the church, and the preachers. "They would have you believe that God hates sex. But I'm telling you that spirituality of sexuality transforms men and women into gods and goddesses."

UNCLE YAH YAH: PART 2
21st Century Man of Wisdom

HOW TO SEX

I CAN'T CLOSE THIS SUBJECT WITHOUT giving some helpful hints on the 'How To Of Sex.' In the book The Greatest Power in the Universe by U.S. Anderson it says, 'Orgasm is one of the most important and powerful rhythms of life. The whole living world is subject to it. Orgasmic discharge clears away neuroses and brings the full use of mental power. Built up energy is discharged by healthy orgasm. It expresses every human emotion. It is life in miniature expressing the dynamics of living.'

"Orgasm in men and women is similar. In both, it is the reflex that releases muscular tension and reverses the flow of blood to the pelvic area. Women require stimulation up to and throughout orgasm. Men are different, stimulated to the point of no return, orgasm will occur even if stimulation stops. In women, the second stimulation stops, even if orgasm is taking place, excitement declines.

"Women have many orgasmic responses. Most men have only one. Women, most of the time, experience contractions during orgasm. There is no one right way, everyone is different. After ejaculation or orgasm, the body returns to normal. You can't force orgasm; it is a natural occurrence. Excitement, plateau, orgasm and resolution are always present in orgasms. "Trained to control ejaculation, men can experience the same orgasm, even multiple orgasms that women feel. Orgasm releases the blood to circulate.

"COMMUNICATION: There are some things we all just can't agree on that is especially true of sex. The first and most important issue is communication. If you don't talk about what your sexual preferences are, and how you wish to be stimulated, only trouble can result. Don't expect your partner to be a mind reader. You can be turning him or her off and thinking you are turning them on. No two people are the same. You really have to spell it all out in detail. Do you like to be touched and kissed? Well then, where and

UNCLE YAH YAH: PART 2
21st Century Man of Wisdom

how? Never force any sex act on your partner. This is one area where no, means no! If it is something you want, and your partner is against it, you can talk about it, but never force it!

"SELF EXPLORATION OR MASTURBATION" is greatly misunderstood. You have no sexual preferences until you learn just what it is that feels good to you. You should not be afraid to try and stimulate your body to discover what excites you to orgasm or ejaculation. How many poor folks have lost a whole lifetime of pleasure because they were taught not to touch their genitals? They said (the ignorant), that hair would grow in the palms of your hands, and you would go blind if you masturbated. Hog wash! You need to experiment, so you can communicate your sexuality to your partner. Only then can you be assured of satisfaction.

"WOMEN have many sensitive and sexually responsive areas. There are the earlobes, neck, breasts, thighs, clitoris and the vagina, just to name a few. Men, for the large part, have the penis as their main responsive area. The male penis and the testicles are sensitive, but even so, there is a special massage, which is very effective. This

UNCLE YAH YAH: PART 2
21st Century Man of Wisdom

effectiveness varies with the individual. It is the same with women. Everyone is different, therefore, a different approach and method is necessary.

"KEEPING IT ALIVE" is another important thing. To know what and how your partner likes to be stimulated is not enough. The monotony of the same old kisses, hugs, and hump hump, gets boring. You need to find new ways, new positions, new places, and new times to have your sex. Make up games. Fulfill fantasies. Learn to act out different roles, like the Big Bad Wolf rapes Little Red Riding Hood, if it is thought stimulating. The point is finding new ways to do what you and your partner like to do.

"HOW TO ACHIEVE it is not simple. Once you are stimulating your partner in the way that excites them, you must keep that rhythm and consistency. This is, until the point of no return for men, and all the way through orgasm, non-stop, for women. Build excitement through foreplay, which is doing all the kissing and touching in the way that the partner likes.

"BEST POSITIONS are the ones which allow freedom of movement and no strain. The less strain the more you can concentrate on the

UNCLE YAH YAH: PART 2
21st Century Man of Wisdom

stimulation. Go with the positions you like, but don't get stuck in a rut with one position. Mix it up, try a variety of positions. One of the best positions is the female on top, because it allows for the stimulation of the vagina and clitoris at the same time.

"MULTIPLE ORGASMS vary from person to person. They are not the rule. Some women experience one real powerful orgasm, while others may experience many small ones. Some can have one, and in a minute or two, have another one as big or bigger. Some will have to take a little time to recuperate. Men, on the other hand, can in some cases have one orgasm and move right on to having another, with their penis remaining erect. However, most men need time to recuperate after a strong orgasm.

"SEX DURING PREGNANCY is fine, and can continue in most cases right up to a few days before delivery. Check with your physician. You need to be careful by using positions which do not put pressure on the stomach. Rear entry is very good for advanced pregnancy; it avoids strain. Sex during pregnancy is very good; just take it easy.

"Sexual age begins at puberty and stops at the grave. There are people 80 and 90 years old who are sexually active and loving every minute of it.

"SEX HYGIENE is very important. The cleaner you and your partner are the better your sex. Psychologically, you feel more comfortable with a partner who has just had a complete bath. If you have the slightest body odor, it detracts from the pleasure. That is, unless your thing is foul body odors. It is good for your partner to witness the bath, so take a bath or shower together. It builds confidence, it also helps to protect against venereal disease.

"VIRGINITY is a special time in your life, and it is a difficult time. Partners should be considerate and patient. Women, in some cases, experience great pain in the initial breaking of the hymen. If there is a lot of pain, I suggest the use of KY jelly. Some women are virgins without hymens. For them, the first experience is a bit easier. The rule is, take your time! As for the man, he may experience great fear. That is, he may feel that he may not be able to perform or give pleasure to his partner. Same rule, take your time and take it one step at a time! Just stay with the foreplay and don't worry about going all the way. Once pressure to perform is set aside, nature will do the rest.

UNCLE YAH YAH: PART 2
21st Century Man of Wisdom

So relax and take your time.

"THE BEST POSITIONS FOR PROCREATION are the ones that allow you to penetrate the vagina the deepest. The rear entry is very good for making babies. The missionary position with the man on the top, and the woman's knees pulled back as far as they will go, also allows deep penetration.

"FANTASY plays a major role in all of our sexual experience. Don't be ashamed of your fantasies. Look at every detail of them, and they will reveal to you that which excites you the most.

"AFTER SEX, men usually want to roll over and go to sleep. Women, on the other hand, are ready for hugs and kisses. This is their time for closeness. Men should prepare for this time and not jump up or go to sleep. This time after sex can really be reassuring for a relationship if you let it. It is a time for true romance.

"BAD SEX is anal sex. It leads to AIDS and other diseases. Sex during the menstrual cycle. Sex when you are unclean and smelly, and any sex that your partner does not want or agree to.

"THE HIGHEST FORMS OF SEXUAL INTERCOURSE is for spiritual advancement, procreation, sexual healing, and the strengthening of each other. If you start with a good clean bath and a prayer of thanks to God (keeping this reverence during copulation), and concluding with prayer, you will be spiritually uplifted. You and your partner can decide to procreate at will. If your communication is as it should be as the woman's orgasm approaches, the male should position himself so that he can enter the vagina as far as he can. You both must think and hold the thought of the male or female child you want. You can, if practical, orgasm and ejaculate at the same time, or one after the other, but hold the thought. Try it and see! Another helpful hint in choosing gender lies in the woman's vaginal fluid. If it has a salty odor her body's make-up is conducive to conceiving a male child. If the vaginal fluid has a sweetish odor it is conducive to a female child. Healing occurs every time you have sex. The stronger heals the weaker!

"APHRODISIACS: Are best left alone!"

UNCLE YAH YAH: PART 2
21st Century Man of Wisdom

POLYGAMY

A YOUNG WOMAN SITTING AT the small table to the left of the dance floor raised her hand.

Uncle Yah Yah acknowledged her by saying, "We have a question from the audience. Stand up, young lady." The pretty girl stood up.

"We don't usually take questions from the floor, but you look so pretty and I'm sure you have a good question for me, so I'll break with tradition just for you. What is your question?" Uncle Yah Yah asked.

"What do you think of polygamy? That is, a man having more than one wife?" she asked as she sat down.

Uncle Yah Yah smiled as he glanced over the audience, and let his gaze rest on the pretty young lady. He began, "In this country it is against the law to have more than one wife, but in most of the world's civilizations this practice is common. "Having a history that goes back as far as man, polygamy has proven its usefulness and great value to society. However, in this country, there is the idea that only sex fiends would live in a polygamous relationship. "If you take sex out of the picture, what do you have left? You have a nuclear family working together for the benefit of all its members. Care for the husband is shared, care for the children is shared, and the household chores are also shared. In fact, all is shared. "So, the best work can be expected from each member because no one is over burdened. "Think of the millions of housewives who wish they could call on a companion to help feed the baby, clean the bathroom, or just be company.

"Polygamy brings out the best in women and men. Also, the children are more responsive to authority because all the adults help supervise them. They receive instruction and attention from several mothers and a father.

"The women, in a polygamous marriage, must maintain and cultivate a positive attitude. They must guard against petty jealousy, greediness, and selfishness. They must keep a level head in order to share everything, including their husband. That takes a great character. A woman will have to want for her sister co-wife what she wants for herself.

"The man, in a polygamous marriage, is elevated to the King of his castle and the Lord of his people. He must be just by treating everyone the same, and at the same time tend to everyone's needs. He must be successful in all his undertakings. He must be a master at thinking and planning his family's survival. He is their protector, spiritual guide, and teacher. He must express a divine character at all times, or his household will fall apart.

"No weak man can control the lives of several people if he can't control himself. If out of lust the weakling should try to manage three or four wives, he will kill himself in a week's time.

"Polygamy destroys prostitution and thus reduces social diseases. A nation is no stronger than its smallest unit, the family. Polygamy produces the strongest family unit.

"There are other great benefits to this type of union. Some say, and I agree, it is the quickest way to become God-like, or in the image of God, their Supreme Being.

UNCLE YAH YAH: PART 2
21st Century Man of Wisdom

"Because of all the good in the practice of polygamy, this country should give people the option of polygamy or monogamy. It will also solve the problem of women out numbering men by 7 to 1, and it will be by 11 to 1 in the year 2002.

"The church is the strongest opposition to polygamy. But that's nothing new. The church hates sex. Why?

"Last but not least, polygamy provides a way for widows and orphans to become a vital part of an indigenous family unit, and gives them a social identity and status which they can be proud of."

UNCLE YAH YAH: PART 2
21st Century Man of Wisdom

AIDS

ANOTHER DARK SUITED MAN, who was sitting on the opposite side of the long table, raised his hand. "What do you think about AIDS?" he asked.

"There is still a lot of mystery about AIDS," Uncle Yah Yah answered. "Its origin, transmission, and prevention are for the greater part still somewhat mysterious. There is still no cure. Once you get it, your days on this earth are numbered. Treatment for AIDS patients is still in the developmental stages.

"I have heard a lot of theories, but the one which got my attention was a Russian report stating that the American CIA produced this disease in its military laboratory for germ warfare. And that the attempt to test the effects of the germ on homosexuals and intravenous drug users, somehow got out of hand and began to spread.

UNCLE YAH YAH: PART 2
21st Century Man of Wisdom

"I am told that South Africa's president, Botha, introduced the germ among the Black population in order to decrease the number of the Black majority. Today, there are millions of Blacks in Africa with the AIDS infection. Homosexuality has been around for thousands of years, but AIDS just came to the public's awareness within the last decade. Someone put it there!

"AIDS has scared the general public into thinking twice before becoming intimate with anyone. People are not so quick to hug and kiss anymore. No one is trying to catch this stuff."

UNCLE YAH YAH: PART 2
21st Century Man of Wisdom

PSYCHIC SCIENCES

"IS THERE ANY TRUTH TO MENTAL TELEPATHY?" One of the Companions in a dark suit asked.

"There was a time when we were all gods," Uncle Yah Yah began. "We were taller than the Watusi people, averaging ten feet in height. Our mental powers were like those of super men. We could see through walls, we could fly, we could swim under water like fish, and we could put our bodies into suspended animation or hibernation, for long periods of time. We could walk through a raging fire without being burned. We could read the minds of those near to us or far away. We could send telepathic messages to each other, and distance did not matter.

"It is said that we built the great pyramids of Egypt with our collective physic powers. That the building bricks were all cut exactly

UNCLE YAH YAH: PART 2
21st Century Man of Wisdom

alike having an average weight of 2,500 pounds. The type of granite used came from a mountain about 1,000 miles away. It was mind power that transported those huge stones. Then they were stacked on top of one another with an exact fit, all on a foundation of sand, which is said to have no foundation. This was done at a time when modern building equipment had yet to be invented. Did you know that an atomic light was found in a secret chamber of one of the great pyramids?

"As man lost his knowledge of the True and Living God, which is in him, he lost his god- power. Today, we don't even use a fraction of our animal mind, and none of our god-powers. The average person thinks mind power is a joke or some kind of magician's trick. It is something babies are naturally born with, but culture takes it from them.

"The methods of telepathy is easy to learn. The practice and the discipline is that which will make or break you. I will give you one of the methods I have used for years with great success and satisfaction. But before I teach you how to read the minds of others, and send and receive messages at a distance, let me give you some important advice.

"Don't take this ability lightly. It is a God

given talent. If you use it properly, it will open the door to greater power and god-like characteristics. Your greatest joy will be to help uplift fallen humanity. On the other hand, if you misuse this ability by becoming a psychic peeping tom, entering where you have not been invited, invading privacy and selling your ability for a few dollars, or in any way taking unlawful advantage of your fellow man, you will lose your ability. Also, depending on how serious the violation, you could destroy yourself. So don't fool around with this. Be sincere and dependent on God's guidance and you will do just fine. Fools march in where angels fear to tread.

"So with that said, let's do it! The first thing you need is a strong mind to be successful. The mind is strengthened by methods of concentration. The best method of concentrated power is prayer. The next step is a relaxing exercise. Sit comfortably with your spine straight. Stiffen your feet, holding them that way for five seconds, and then relax them. Next, stiffen your legs, hold it for five seconds, and then relax them. Do the thighs, the buttocks, the diaphragm, the arms and the shoulders, all in their turn. Next, you must breathe deep. Inhale slowly until it feels like you can't get any more air into your lungs. Then exhale slowly until all the air is out. Don't hold your breath. Take another as soon as you feel empty. Do that seven times. At that point, if you don't feel totally relaxed, repeat the process until you do.

"Close your eyes, and keeping your head straight. Visualize a blue ball about the size of a handball. You will find that the mind is very rebellious, but don't strain, be persistent. The mind, like an old friend, will come around eventually and out of curiosity will want to see what you are up to. It will cooperate. Sometimes it happens fast and sometimes slowly. Sometimes you can see the ball very clearly, and at other times it won't be so clear. However, when you are able to see the blue ball whenever you want to, then you are ready to go to the next step.

"Try to find a place where your experiments won't be disturbed, and don't discuss this with people who don't believe in this. Always practice at the same time, and don't practice longer than one half hour at a time, until you have learned and completed all the steps.

"Go through the same preparations, but instead of closing your eyes keep them open.

UNCLE YAH YAH: PART 2
21st Century Man of Wisdom

Visualize the blue ball on the wall from a distance of six to ten feet away. Practice until you can produce the ball at a moment's notice, simply by saying, 'Blue ball,' and having it appear. Then practice getting the ball to appear without the relaxing exercise. When you have accomplished that, you are then ready to read minds, send, and receive messages at a distance (mental telepathy).

"If you have practiced as instructed you are now powerful enough to tune in on anyone, anywhere.

"Here it is. Visualize the blue ball. This first step is called receiving. The person you wish to receive an impression of, or from, should be aware of your experiment and know about the time set for the experiment. They should write down generally what they are doing at that time.

"At the right time you must visualize the blue ball, and at the same time, you should see a picture of your helper in the center of the ball, like a picture on a TV screen. While holding the picture in the ball say, 'I want to see what (he or she) is doing and thinking.' At that point, you let the thought go. Just stop and think about something else.

"Have a pencil and paper ready, because

after you take your thoughts off the picture in the ball, you will receive some real clear impressions of your friend, and of what they are doing and thinking. Write it down exactly as revealed. Don't allow yourself to rationalize. Write what you see and hear just as it comes. Don't add or take from it, even if it looks or sounds crazy. Repeat the experiment a few times in a sitting and then compare notes with your friend.

"Your first success at this is a powerful thing. Don't get big-headed; you are still just a baby at this. You need to take your time and practice until you can suggest that you want to know the thoughts, or see the whereabouts of anyone, and it will happen. With the above accomplished, you can move on to the last and hardest step. That is, sending your thoughts to a target person.

"The process changes a little when you want to send a thought. First, you visualize the blue ball, imagining it as a tube-like tunnel through which you can see a light at its end. Then you make a picture of the message you are going to send. Next, you must imagine you are traveling down that tunnel at a high speed toward the light at its end. You must now visualize the person and the message you are sending. Then as you come out of the blue tunnel and into the light, you are bathed in a beautiful red sunset. You must will that the person receive the message. You must become emotional in reverence of natural beauty, in order to energize, and will the thought to the person. The targeted person usually thinks the thought came from them. They, the receiver, should keep an open or receptive mind at the time of the experiment and write down all their impressions during that time.

"Once you learn to energize the thought at the end of the blue tunnel, the rest is easy. After you visualize the person and emotionally will the thought to them, you then take your mind off the experiment. This allows the thought to be released. As long as you hold it in your mind it can't go anywhere, so visualize and then turn it loose.

"Practice, practice, practice! That is the key."

UNCLE YAH YAH: PART 2
21st Century Man of Wisdom

THE EGYPTIAN BOOK OF THE DEAD

"UNCLE YAH YAH, CAN YOU TELL us anything about the Egyptian Book of the Dead?" was the next question asked.

"Yes, The Egyptian Book of the Dead is a very powerful book, but it is one of the most misunderstood books in the world today. However, I am blessed to be one of the few people instructed with the key to unlock the secret of this great book. I will tell it to you.

"In ancient times when a pharaoh or king of Egypt died, the high priest was responsible for seeing that the pharaoh's spirit found its way across the river of death, to reach the kingdom of paradise in the other world. These instructions were so important that the walls of the burial tomb were painted with them. The pharaoh was buried with all the provisions he would need for the journey. That is, a ship, clothes, food, money, and servants. To make sure that he did not misunderstand the written instructions inscribed on all the walls of his tomb, the pharaoh would take a good number of priests with him just to be sure.

"The pharaoh's spirit was warned of the dangers now lying in his path, and how to overcome these demons, traps, scorpions, and poisonous vipers. The Book of the Dead gave him specific instructions for the just dead and the disoriented spirit. Once the spirit acknowledged that it was no longer a part of this world, it was then free to start its journey across the river. On the path, the spirit must be armed with wisdom and the worship of the God, to defeat the evil forces against it. If he, the pharaoh's spirit, became weak or fearful, he would not make it. He had to keep good sense and faith at all times, until he arrived at the Place of God.

"At the time of death, a priest would address the spirit like this, 'O great pharaoh, you have passed over to the other side. This is no longer your home. Don't be afraid to leave. Don't hold on to the things of this world. They are no longer yours. Look to the light, and prepare for your journey through the other world, until you reach the kingdom. Leave those things now O noble spirit. Go now and keep your face to the light. You are not among us anymore.'

"Once the spirit is departed it must then be prepared for a journey full of trials. It is a beautiful book and it is full of wisdom.

"The key to the proper understanding is that you must follow those instructions now, while you are alive! We are all on a journey to God's kingdom while we are alive. When we recognize that we are ignorant (mentally dead), we can then leave that lowly state of existence. Take up the wisdom of truth, which will take you through the valleys of the shadow of death in your everyday living experience. If we hold onto the guidance of God, and keep the faith, our journey will be safe until we become one with God.

"Yes, this book is for the living. We have all the demons, snakes, and scorpions, along with lying hypocrites that any of us will ever confront right now. We need those instructions now! Remember, 'An alive dog is better than a dead king.' No one will come back after the physical death. Your journey to heaven through hell is right now while you live.

UNCLE YAH YAH: PART 2
21st Century Man of Wisdom

"There is also a sister book, The Tibetan Book of the Dead.

"There is no pie in the sky after we die. Heaven and hell are right here and now. To know this is to be alive and on your journey to God. To not know this is to be ignorant, a dead head."

UNCLE YAH YAH: PART 2
21st Century Man of Wisdom

BLACK NATIONALISM

"CAN YOU DEFINE BLACK Nationalism for us?" was the next question put to Uncle Yah Yah?

"It is a truism that what goes up must come down. History is always played by those at the top and those at the bottom. A government is like the human body. When you take care of your body, you live longer and the quality of life is good and disease free. So it is with the government body.

"When the government body fails to care for its parts, when it abuses its parts, that body becomes diseased. Dissatisfaction, unrest, insurrection, chaos and anarchy are the natural result of bad government policies or lifestyles. Diseases!

UNCLE YAH YAH: PART 2
21st Century Man of Wisdom

"It doesn't matter what a government's title is, democracy, monarchy, socialism, or communism; call it what you want. The fact is, you must feed, clothe, and house your people. Failure to do that subjects that government body to disease and eventually death.

"Nationalism is coming about because of its timeliness. Nothing is greater than an idea in its time.

"If people need jobs and food, they blame the government. A diseased body progressively gets worst until all body functions are broken down.

"There are fifty million black people in this country. If they are not cared for, they will find a way to feed and provide for self.

"Racism, on the other hand, is a different thing when applied to the black people who are descendants of slaves. Racism is not a bad thing when it results in forming love and unity of one's own kind. Every nation should be proud of its race and should compete to be the best in all it does.

"However, Blacks have always been brainwashed into believing that we were not like other people, that we have no nation or ethnic purity. That is why the call to nationhood is so attractive to the Blacks in

UNCLE YAH YAH: PART 2
21st Century Man of Wisdom

America today.

"The Blacks are suffering from the greatest of neglect, abuse and are highly dissatisfied. It is inevitable that government change to give them a fair share, or they will discover or create a way to feed and provide jobs for themselves.

"Thomas Jefferson (third president of the U.S.) described the situation of America's Blacks like this, 'It is still in our power to direct the process of emancipation and deportation of the (Negro Slave) peaceably, and in such a slow degree that the evil will wear off insensibly; and their places will be Pari passu (on equal footing), filled up by free white laborers. If, on the contrary, it is left to force itself on, human nature must shudder at the prospect held up.'

"Truer words couldn't have been spoken. We were Negroes and colored people in the fifties and early sixties, and in the late sixties and seventies we were Black and Proud. In the eighties we were Black Nationalist and descendants of Africa, the richest continent on the planet.

"This is the natural course of history. It cannot be manufactured or forced. If the conditions for complete dissatisfaction are not

UNCLE YAH YAH: PART 2
21st Century Man of Wisdom

present, there will be no change. If America cares for her poor and needy, the poor and needy will uphold the government.

"Che Guevara went into Bolivia and tried to implant revolution, but the people were not dissatisfied. It is said that some goat farmers told the government troops where Che was hiding because they said he was teaching the peasants to use firearms, which was frightening the goats. As a result of that, the goat's milk production had fallen off.

"So it is all a natural process. When the time for a change is right, nature produces the people to bring that change about.

"Before I close this subject, let me say a little about White Supremacy. First, you must understand that the European white man is the minority on the planet. He is vastly outnumbered by the Black, Brown, Yellow and Red people. If he doesn't keep himself separate from mixing with the darker people of the earth, he will be history in a very few years. In order to keep his race pure, he must have power to control and be in a superior position to Blacks. He must teach and practice white supremacy.

"His schools and religion dominate and indoctrinate the darker people of the earth to accept white as better than everyone else.

"The minute white people establish equality and brotherhood with Blacks, history will record that once upon a time there was a white man on earth, and he ruled the world for a thousand years."

UNCLE YAH YAH: PART 2
21st Century Man of Wisdom

THE PARTY AFTER THE PARTY

I WAS DRUNK FROM HEARING SO much wisdom. I had a few things I wanted to ask Uncle Yah Yah, but I wasn't sure it would be proper for me to ask at this time. Maybe I better wait, I thought.

Uncle Yah Yah seemed to be really enjoying himself. He was looking for the next question when suddenly, the man with the microphone stood up and said. "That's about it for the questions for tonight. Let's give Uncle Yah Yah a break. If the man doesn't eat soon, he might try to eat that shoe he mentioned. So let's give him a big round of applause for blessing us with great enlightenment tonight. And now, it's time to party!"

The crowd was on its feet for three minutes or more, and did not stop clapping until the

UNCLE YAH YAH: PART 2
21st Century Man of Wisdom

band drowned them out with their rendition of "Celebration Time."

I passed the tape I'd recorded to Uncle Yah Yah and asked if I could speak with him about some personal matters in a day or two. He said, "Sure, come over to the house any time you like." I thanked him, shook his hand, and started off to find the table where Freda and Dottie were seated.

Someone touched my arm. It was Aunt Willie Mae, Yah Yah's wife. She said, "Mr. Hawkins, welcome back. I hope you enjoy your stay. Here is the little book that Uncle Yah Yah wrote while he was in his cabin for forty days. I hope you like it." With that said, she handed me a legal size brown envelope and disappeared in the crowd.

I found Dottie and Freda right where they said they would be. Both were bubbling with excitement. I was too. We looked at each other and laughed. "I don't ever remember being this happy," I said to them.

"Me too," they both chimed in.

"Look what Aunt Willie Mae gave me," I said as I pulled the latest manuscript of Uncle Yah Yah's out of the envelope.

"Let's go read it," Freda said with eyes open wide.

UNCLE YAH YAH: PART 2
21st Century Man of Wisdom

Dottie said, "Yeah, let's do that."

I surprisingly said, "Now, tonight!"

"Yes. Let's go up to your cabin, the three of us, and be the first to read this. I know it is full of blessings," Freda said.

I said, "Okay, let's go."

We had just made it to my cabin door, and as I was putting the key in the lock, up walked Sue and her husband, Brother-in-law Dear. "Hey, what are you two doing up here, and why aren't you at the party?" I asked.

"Because we want to hear what's in the book Uncle Yah Yah wrote," Sue said.

"How did you know about that?" I asked.

"Aunt Willie Mae told us she gave it to you," Sue answered. We all laughed and went inside. We decided that each one of us could take turns reading aloud. I was to be the first.

"Everybody ready?" I asked.

"Yes, we are if you are," Sue said. I took the little book out of the envelope and started to read.

UNCLE YAH YAH: PART 2
21st Century Man of Wisdom

THE SECOND MANUSCRIPT
by
UNCLE YAH YAH

UNCLE YAH YAH: PART 2
21st Century Man of Wisdom

UNCLE YAH YAH: PART 2
21st Century Man of Wisdom

THE BEGINNING

LIKE THE BEE, I HAVE COLLECTED nectar from many sources. The many simple truths in this little book are like honey. It is strength and a healing for you. What is written on these pages is very important. It is the guidance that will get you through life's ups and downs.

Don't let the simplicity, and sometimes absurdity of these little animal stories fool you. They carry a very potent message. These maxims, parables, proverbs and wise sayings come from some of the finest minds that ever lived. Even God Himself is quoted in this little book.

The difference in having the wisdom in this book, and not having it, can be illustrated by the man who is about to kill himself. If he knew that at the moment of his death he would awaken in a new body, but with the same circumstances he just left, having that knowledge the man wouldn't kill himself. He would face up to the problem with courage, seeking to overcome it, especially when he realizes that there is no way out, and that he had to face it.

The truth, thought of or spoken at the right time, saves lives. So look for the message and don't be concerned with the method of delivery. If you get the message, that is what counts.

In the beginning, God and His sons lived in a garden of paradise. They were all powerful. They did not sleep or eat, and they knew neither sickness nor death. They were ever-living and self-subsisting. They lived in complete peace and contentment in the presence of Almighty God.

There came a time when the Lord called for all His sons to be present for an important meeting. They all took their places at the right hand of God. But there was one who sat himself on the left-hand side of God. The Lord understood this creation.

"What do you want here, devil?" the Lord asked.

"You know what I want," came the reply.

UNCLE YAH YAH: PART 2
21st Century Man of Wisdom

"I want to show up these fools you call your precious sons as hypocrites and weaklings. I will turn them away from you and make them love the dark side. This is my time, so give me your blessings and I will deceive them all."

"I am your Lord and I am their Lord, so do what you will. I now give you power over their souls. So go and work your work. You have a time, time and a half of a time. Then I will come after them to restore them to paradise. Then too, I will chain you up and cast you into the fiery dungeon of hell, never to be freed again."

The devil cast a spell on the sons of God, causing them to drift into a deep sleep. He then transported them to the underworld of material things. When he awakened them, they found themselves naked and in a hot desert.

"Where is the Lord, and what is this place?" the sons asked.

"This is the real world, my domain," the devil said. "Your good Lord has forsaken you. He has left you here at my mercy. He is in His garden paradise hiding from you," the devil said, laughing and mocking the sons of the Lord.

"Yes, He has forsaken you. Only I can help you now. I can teach you how to get nourishment, how to clothe and shelter yourself for a price. I can even show you how to find your way back to the paradise you just lost," the devil told them with a cunning grin on his face.

The sons, feeling helpless and frustrated, said, "All right, what do you want us to do?"

The above story is the ancient account of the beginning of the Spiritual Dark Age, the Rein of Evil. The devil knew that once he could trick us into believing that God was outside of us, instead of inside us, he could make us believe he knew the way to find God. That was the beginning of organized sin, better known as so-called religion. Any religion that teaches that God is outside of man, is of the devil. There is no God outside of man, and no man outside of God.

The return of God is the return of the knowledge that God is within each and every one of us. When we study God's words of Wisdom, we learn to recognize His voice within our hearts and within our souls. Once we are put back in touch with God, the devil has no more power over us. Those of us who have found the way back to the garden of the Lord, within us, are obligated to pass the direction on to our fellow man. Speak the truth regardless! Sometimes a phrase or a word will turn on the mental switch, which will light up the path back to the Throne of God within us.

Never pass up the opportunity to teach the truth. This little book will free you from the devil's tricks, and teach you how to manifest the Supreme Being in You.

UNCLE YAH YAH: PART 2
21st Century Man of Wisdom

THE MONKEY AND THE SNAKE

A troop of monkeys were grooming themselves in the midday sun, and hiding in the shade of the leafy branches created in the top of the trees. All seemed well enough, until Junior, the monkey spotted a snake stretched out on a tree limb.

"A snake, a snake!" Junior cried out. The troop leader sounded the alarm, and the troops began to move away from the danger. That is, all but Junior. He let curiosity get the best of him. He slowly sneaked up close to the tree branch until he was now close enough to touch it.

The troops began to yell, "Junior, get away from that snake. It will kill you."

Junior had noticed the snake's tail hanging

UNCLE YAH YAH: PART 2
21st Century Man of Wisdom

off the branch. He thought he could pull the snake's tail and dislodge it from the limb.

"Junior, you'd better get away from there," the troop continued to warn.

Just then he reached out and grabbed the boa constrictor by its tail and gave it a good jerk. But before Junior could turn the tail loose, the snake coiled itself around Junior's wrist. Realizing that he was caught, Junior began to scream, "Help me, help me. Somebody please help me."

The troop moved away slowly, knowing that was the end of Junior.

Remember: ALL OF OUR HARDSHIPS ARE SELF-IMPOSED. SIMPLY STATED, "IF YOU MAKE YOUR BED HARD, YOU ARE THE ONE WHO HAS TO SLEEP IN IT."

-End-

UNCLE YAH YAH: PART 2
21st Century Man of Wisdom

MALLARD THE DUCK

Mallard the Duck had inherited a beautiful mansion. He and his new bride had only been in residence one week when they began to argue and fight like drunken sailors.

The Community Council could stand no more. So they chose a representative to go ask the Ducks to move out. Their neighbors all had filed complaints against them. But before the representative could carry out his mission, the noise from the mansion mysteriously stopped. Now the community became suspicious and afraid that the Ducks might have killed each other in a fit of anger.

They decided to send an investigator to find out what was going on. The investigator rang the doorbell, and Mrs. Duck answered the

UNCLE YAH YAH: PART 2
21st Century Man of Wisdom

door.

"What do you want?" she asked.

The investigator replied, "I am looking for your husband. Is he home?"

"Yes, he is out back. He doesn't like living in a mansion like real people," Mrs. Duck said.

The investigator went out back and saw a little tent, and in it was Mr. Duck. So the investigator asked, "Why are you living in this tent instead of your mansion?"

"BECAUSE IT IS BETTER TO LIVE IN PEACE IN A TENT, THAN TO LIVE IN A MANSION WITH A TYRANT," answered Mallard the Duck.

-End-

UNCLE YAH YAH: PART 2
21st Century Man of Wisdom

THE FROG AND THE GENIE

A poor frog was sitting on a lily pad crying the blues. "I ain't got nobody, and all I see is hard luck and trouble," he moaned.

"Hey Frog," said a voice from out of nowhere. The frog looked all around him, but couldn't determine where the voice had come from.

"Hey Frog, look down here," the voice said again.

The frog looked down into the water and saw a light. "What in the world is this?" said the frog.

"Swim down here and I'll give you a blessing," the voice said.

The frog dove into the water and swam toward the light. To the frog's surprise, he

UNCLE YAH YAH: PART 2
21st Century Man of Wisdom

found a bottle with a tiny little man standing inside of it. The little man was wearing a sleeping gown and a cap, and in his hand he held a little lit candle.

"Who are you, and what are you doing in here?" asked the frog.

"I am a genie, and I have been in this bottle for one hundred years. If you take the cork stopper off and let me out, I will give you four magic sticks."

The frog said, "This must be my lucky day," as he opened the bottle.

The genie popped out stretching and yawning, and said, "Thank you ever so much. Now here are your magic sticks. Each stick will give you whatever your heart desires. All you have to do is make a wish and break a stick, but the last stick you must never break."

The frog was so happy as he held the sticks in his hand. He just had to see if they really worked. He made a wish for a plate full of juicy flies and quickly broke the first stick. To his amazement there appeared, right in front of him, a plate of flies.

As he started to eat the flies with relish, the genie said, "Good-bye. Don't forget to save the last stick. Never break it." And with those words of caution the genie disappeared.

UNCLE YAH YAH: PART 2
21st Century Man of Wisdom

The frog was now ready to ask for his next blessing. He made a wish to be young and handsome; then he broke the second stick, and sure enough he was now young and handsome. The frog looked at the two sticks left, and decided that he would wish for all that a frog could want to be happy for the rest of his life. He then broke the third stick.

He was then a king among frogs, and his domain was a beautiful pond with golden lily pads. The frog was so impressed with the richness of all he had, that he began to wonder, "If one stick could produce all that wealth, what would happen if I broke the last stick? I bet I could become as great as the genie himself."

The frog then made a wish and broke the fourth stick. Suddenly, with a loud bang and a puff of smoke, the frog found himself on the same lily pad he was on before he met the genie, and just as poor.

UNCLE YAH YAH: PART 2
21st Century Man of Wisdom

DON'T BE GREEDY AND NOTHING WILL SWALLOW YOU UP. MODERATION IS THE KEY."
-End-

UNCLE YAH YAH: PART 2
21st Century Man of Wisdom

THE GOAT AND THE SHEEP

A goat and a sheep were having a serious debate about paradise. The goat said, "It ain't no such thing. It's just an old wives' tale, and you are silly to believe that stuff." Confident that this argument would prevail, he returned to chewing on a clump of bushes.

"It is too," the sheep said, showing a little bewilderment.

The goat snapped back, "Who you know ever come back to tell you about it, if you so smart?"

"I don't know anybody, but I just believe that paradise does exist," the sheep said in a quiet voice.

Right then an angel of the Lord came walking by and the goat said, "Now we can get a good opinion." The goat called out, "Hey Angel, is there such a thing as paradise for real?"

The Angel said, "Of course, I just left there.

The bridge is just a little way down the road. If you like I will show it to you."

So the goat and the sheep went with the Angel, until they came to the bridge. The Angel said, "Here it is. Want me to show you across?"

"Yes, oh yes, please do," said the sheep hardly able to contain his joy.

But the goat had a worried look on his face. "Uh, is this bridge safe?" he asked, as he cautiously followed the angel and the sheep onto the bridge.

Midway across the bridge the sheep was filled with such a heavenly spirit he shouted, "Praise the Lord, the Highest. I see it. There it is. O Glory," then ran to the other side.

The goat stopped, looked around, and said, "I'm going back. I smell the smoke of hell."

The angel said, "AS YOU SEE IT, THAT'S HOW IT IS FOR YOU. YOU GET WHAT YOU LOOK FOR."

-End-

UNCLE YAH YAH: PART 2
21st Century Man of Wisdom

THE SKUNK AND DEATH

Oliver Skunk did not believe in fate and fortune telling. He felt that man determined his own destiny. So when Mo Joe, the fortune telling raven, told Oliver that he was going to die at 8 P.M. that night, Oliver flew into a rage and told the raven to get out of his house, and to take his dumb tarot cards with him.

Nonetheless, Oliver Skunk then took steps to protect himself from death. After he boarded up all the windows and doors, he then felt secure.

He thought to himself, "Ain't nothing getting in here now," as he laughed, got a book, and sat down in front of his warm fireplace. The heat was soothing and he soon fell fast asleep. At about eight o'clock that

UNCLE YAH YAH: PART 2
21st Century Man of Wisdom

evening, Oliver Skunk died of asphyxiation. The poisonous carbon monoxide had built up creating a death trap, because Oliver Skunk had boarded up all the windows and doors. No oxygen could get in.

Just goes to show: WHAT'S FOR YOU, YOU'VE GOT TO GET!

-End-

UNCLE YAH YAH: PART 2
21st Century Man of Wisdom

TAMMY THE CAT

Mrs. Minnie Cat was cursing mad as she prepared to go to the courthouse. Her teenage daughter, Tammy, was going to be arraigned, and Mrs. Cat wanted to try and get her out of jail.

"If I've told that child once, I've told her a hundred times, to stay away from those low-life folks out there in those streets. Her head is so hard. I can't understand her fascination with whores, dope pushers, and gangsters. Now I've got to miss a day's work. I ought to let her stay in jail," she thought as she adjusted her hat, checked her pocketbook, and locked the door as she went out.

When she entered the courthouse, the clerk pointed her to room 104. As Mrs. Cat opened the door, the judge was saying, "Miss Tammy Cat, please stand as I read the charges against

UNCLE YAH YAH: PART 2
21st Century Man of Wisdom

you."

Mrs. Cat took a seat up front so she could hear everything.

The judge said, "This is a code 611 charging you with prostitution and a code 780 charging you with the possession of a narcotic drug. How do you plea?"

Mrs. Cat almost fainted as she said, "Oh no, not my baby!"

"Order in the court," said the judge. "How do you plea to these charges, Miss Tammy Cat?"

"I'm not guilty," said Tammy. "I'm not a prostitute; in fact, I've never been with a man, and I don't use drugs. I was just standing there talking with some of my friends, and the police came and arrested us all."

"Okay, I'm sentencing you to six months in jail, and it's not because you did any of those things, I'M JUDGING YOU BY THE COMPANY YOU KEEP!"

-End-

UNCLE YAH YAH: PART 2
21st Century Man of Wisdom

THE DIK DIK AND THE GIRAFFE

The Dik Dik, smallest of antelopes, and the Giraffe, tallest of animals, were good friends.

One day the Giraffe invited the Dik Dik over to have dinner. The Dik Dik rented a tuxedo and arrived right on time.

"Come in, come in," said the Giraffe. "I was just preparing to eat right now. I hope you have a good appetite," he said as he marched over to a large Acacia tree and began to eat the tender leaves from the uppermost branches.

The poor Dik Dik ran around and around the tree, jumping now and then in hopes of catching a leafy branch. But it was of no use. He could not partake of this meal. He went home with an empty stomach and very disappointed in his friend the Giraffe. So he thought of a plan.

The next day the Dik Dik approached his friend and said, "Good morning, Giraffe. I would like to return a favor and invite you to have dinner with me tonight. I have some of the most succulent Acacia leaves you have ever tasted."

The Giraffe was excited as he ran home to clean up and dress for dinner.

"Come right in," said the Dik Dik. "I was getting ready to eat. Come right this way."

The Dik Dik had spread the tasty sweet leaves on the ground and was lapping them up with relish. But the Giraffe found it too much of a strain to get his head down that low. He spread his legs as far as they would go, but to no avail. Dissatisfied, he went home hungry.

He learned: DON'T DO IT TO OTHERS IF YOU DON'T WANT IT DONE TO YOU!

-End-

UNCLE YAH YAH: PART 2
21st Century Man of Wisdom

THE DOG CATCHER

Joe the dogcatcher came to work depressed as usual. He hated his job at the animal shelter. He was just too much of an animal lover. However, today would prove to be a turning point in his life.

As he was feeding his charges, he came upon a new inmate in number nine cage, and it was love at first sight. This little dog was the most beautiful mutt he had ever seen. The little brown and white dog reminded him of the Walt Disney picture, The Lady and the Tramp; it was about two dogs. This one looked just like Lady.

"Hey Joe," his boss called out to him.

"Yeah," Joe answered. "I'm back here feeding. What do you need?"

UNCLE YAH YAH: PART 2
21st Century Man of Wisdom

"I want you to get that new charge in cage nine ready to be gassed," his boss replied.

Joe felt sick to his stomach as he looked at the little dog, his friend of just a few hours, but yet a strong bond existed between them.

The little dog seemed to know what was happening and began to beg softly, as he pushed his little paws against the door of the cage.

Joe knew what he had to do. He opened the cage door, put Browny, as he had come to call him, inside his coat. He walked through the building to a side exit, opened it, and turned Browny loose. But not before the little dog could give his face a sound licking in gratitude. Browny knew what the deal was, as he ran off like a streak of lightning.

Consequently, Joe was fired from his job, and his life took a down and out turn. He became one of the street people, sleeping in hallways and alleyways, and his only friend was a bottle of wine.

One day Joe found himself on the Brooklyn Bridge. He looked down at the water two or three times but couldn't get up enough courage to jump. He sat down on the bridge, took out his wine bottle, and turned it up to his lips.

He noticed a long white limousine slow

UNCLE YAH YAH: PART 2
21st Century Man of Wisdom

down, pass by him, and then stop and begin to back up to where he sat and parked.

The door opened, and before he could blink an eye, a little brown dog jumped out. It kept jumping up and down, and kept looking back and forth between the limo and Joe sitting there.

An elderly man got out and came over to Joe and said, "You must be a very good friend of my dog, Elmo. I've never seen him act like that toward anyone but me. He made me stop the car when he saw you. I could not contain him. I knew it was important to him that I stop. Now I see what it is."

Joe, by this time, had cleared his head enough to recognize Browny, the little dog whose life he had saved.

The gentleman said, "You look like you can use a job. How about coming to live with me and Elmo? I have a mansion and I will find you a good job. What do you say?"

Hugging Browny, and crying tears of joy, Joe said, "Yes!"

They all got into the car and were happy from then on.

That just goes to show: WHAT GOES AROUND COMES AROUND!

-End -

UNCLE YAH YAH: PART 2
21st Century Man of Wisdom

THE DONKEY'S REVENGE

During the California gold rush days, there lived a wicked old gold miner. One day the old miner went into town to buy some supplies and a donkey.

The old miner went to the stables and found a donkey, but the owner did not want to sell him.

"Why won't you sell me this donkey?" asked the miner.

"Because he's like family. He is a family pet. We couldn't sell him," the owner said.

"I am a gold prospector and I must have this animal. I will pay you three times the asking price in gold," the prospector said.

The owner was a poor man, so he accepted the money for the donkey. But he told the old wicked miner to be good to the donkey

UNCLE YAH YAH: PART 2
21st Century Man of Wisdom

because the donkey was very intelligent and a hard worker.

As soon as the wicked miner got the donkey out of town, he picked up a big stick and began to beat the donkey.

"You see this stick? I'm going to beat you every time you slow me down." He hit the poor donkey. "Don't you look at me like that!" And he hit him again. "I don't care how smart you think you are. I'm the boss and you will do as I say. Do you understand?"

The donkey was very sad because every day the wicked miner would find some excuse to beat him.

One day, just after receiving a beating, the poor donkey was feeling sorry because of his condition. He heard a small voice say to him, "Why do you take such abuse? I saw the whole thing, and you did nothing for which you should be punished."

The donkey looked around to see who was talking to him, and to his surprise, he saw a butterfly sitting on some tumbleweed. "But what can I do?" said the donkey.

"If I were as big and as strong as you, I would wait for a chance to catch him off guard, then I'd jump him," said the butterfly.

"I'll do it. I'll do it!" the donkey said as he

UNCLE YAH YAH: PART 2
21st Century Man of Wisdom

began to hee-haw with glee.

Shortly thereafter, the wicked old miner decided to ride the donkey to town. Along the way, they came to a narrow passage, and the donkey began to run very fast. He then stopped suddenly. This caused the old miner to be thrown off the donkey's back and into a wall. As he lay injured on the ground, the donkey swiftly sat upon him. The miner screamed in pain, and the donkey began to talk to him.

"You have done me wrong. I have never disobeyed you, so now it's my turn, and I'm going to crush your wicked old bones."

The miner cried, "Please, Mr. Donkey, don't kill me. I swear I'll never hit you again. Please forgive me for the wrong I've done. I promise to never be cruel to anyone again. Oh please, Mr. Donkey."

The donkey said, "Okay, but if I ever see your face again, I'm going to crush your bones."

As the donkey trotted off, the butterfly landed on his ear and said, "You won't have to worry about him anymore."

The donkey said, "That was easy. How did you know he would capitulate so easily?"

The butterfly said, "BECAUSE THE

UNCLE YAH YAH: PART 2
21st Century Man of Wisdom

CRUELEST OF MEN ARE THE BIGGEST COWARDS!"

-End-

UNCLE YAH YAH: PART 2
21st Century Man of Wisdom

THE CHICKEN AND THE FOX

Old Ben, Farmer Brown's prize rooster was just about to make his final check of the clock before he would usher in the dawn of a new day with his ever famous cock-a-doodle doo. But before he could utter one sound, he heard a slight noise and turned to see what it was, when BAM! He never saw the culprit who wielded the blunt object that rendered him unconscious.

When Old Ben awoke, he was shocked to find himself surrounded by a bunch of young foxes. Each had a knife in one hand, a fork in the other, and napkins around their necks in anticipation of dinner.

Ben quickly rose to his feet, and with an air of importance and righteous indignation, he asked, "Who is in charge here?"

"I am," came the answer from across the

UNCLE YAH YAH: PART 2
21st Century Man of Wisdom

den.

Ben saw an old fox sitting in a rocking chair, holding a walking stick, smoking a pipe, and looking as sly as a fox can look.

"What can I do for you, Mr. Chicken?" asked the Elder Fox.

Old Ben answered, "I have been brutally assaulted and kidnapped from my home. I know my rights and I demand a speedy hearing and a phone call."

This statement from Ben provoked the young foxes, putting them into a riotous mood. They began rubbing their knives and forks together and shouting obscenities at the chicken.

"You must be out of your mind, fowl," someone shouted. The only rights you got are to taste good when we eat you, and that goes for your mama too," chimed in the voice of another fox.

The young foxes were almost out of hand when the Elder Fox said, "Now, there is no need for all this shouting. Calm down, we are going to eat shortly."

Then looking around the room, Elder Fox asked, "Where is Brother Good Cooking Fox?"

Out of a dark corner of the den came a fox

UNCLE YAH YAH: PART 2
21st Century Man of Wisdom

wearing a chef's hat and apron. "Here I am. I was putting some vegetables and spices in the broth."

"Well, about how much longer before it will be ready?" asked Elder Fox.

"Oh, it won't be too much longer now, about ten more minutes," Brother Good Cooking said.

"Good, then we will hold court for Mr. Chicken while we wait," the Elder Fox said, as he tapped his walking stick on the side of his chair. "You young foxes take a seat over there. I am impaneling you as the jury in this case. Brother Good Cooking Fox will be the prosecutor, and I am the Judge. I assume you will defend yourself. Is that right, Mr. Chicken?"

"Yes sir," said Old Ben with a slight nervous cackle in his voice.

"Okay, this court is now in session. Mr. Chicken, you can give us your statement of the facts," said Elder Fox as he settled back in his chair, more suitable to nodding than listening.

Old Ben spoke up and described the barbarous and savage attack upon his person, the unlawful kidnapping, and his present detention. He spoke at length on the United States Constitution, the Civil Rights Act, of

UNCLE YAH YAH: PART 2
21st Century Man of Wisdom

human rights, and all the national laws, which supported his being acquitted.

Twice Elder Fox interrupted Old Ben to ask Brother Good Cooking if the broth was ready yet, and twice he had to stop the jury from shouting threats at Old Ben.

They were saying things like, "We don't care if you recite every law that was ever written, we still gonna eat your butt tonight," and "You might as well shut-up 'cause you ain't got nothin' comin' here, sucker."

Brother Good Cooking Fox tasted the broth once more and yelled, "Hey, it's ready. All it needs is the chicken!"

The jury was overjoyed. Elder Fox had to be awakened. He said, "All right, Mr. Chicken, we have heard your arguments. We are ready to decide this case. Has the jury a verdict?"

"Yes we do," they all shouted.

"What is your decision?" asked Elder Fox.

One of the young foxes answered, "That Mr. Chicken be plucked and handed over to Brother Good Cooking to prepare as our dinner."

"Good decision. Take him away," ordered Elder Fox.

Old Ben cried out in protest, "What is the meaning of this? I don't understand. What type

UNCLE YAH YAH: PART 2
21st Century Man of Wisdom

of justice is this? You can't do this. I am the victim."

Elder Fox, tying a napkin around his neck said, "It's simple, justice depends on whose house you are in. What would the verdict be if a fox were caught in the hen house?"

WHAT IS JUST TO ONE IS UNJUST TO ANOTHER!

-End-

UNCLE YAH YAH: PART 2
21st Century Man of Wisdom

THE TURTLE AND THE BIG RACE

It was Saturday morning, and time for the big county race. The contestants were ready to start.

Lightning the horse, Lucky the dog, Swifty the mouse and Sloth Foot the turtle were all at the starting line. The crowd was cheering them on and shouting the names of their choice runner.

Every year the county would offer a grand prize of one thousand dollars to the one who could run from one end of the state to the other, 100 miles in three days.

"On your mark, get ready, get set, go!" said Porky Pine as he fired the starter pistol. They were all off to a good start except for Sloth Foot; it looked like he was running in slow motion.

UNCLE YAH YAH: PART 2
21st Century Man of Wisdom

Lightning the horse lived up to his name and was leading the field, with Lucky the dog close behind; and right on the dog's heels was Swifty the mouse. The turtle was somewhere in the rear.

They ran for two days, taking breaks to rest and sleep at night. But Sloth Foot the turtle could not afford a rest, so he kept his pace night and day. Early on the third morning, the horse was up at first light and running fast. He knew he had left the others in the dust. Just then, the road turned through an apple grove.

The horse found himself in the midst of ripe, sweet and juicy apples. He looked around and decided he was so far ahead of the field, he could take a little time out and have an apple or two for breakfast. He ate one and another, and another, until he was so full all he could do was sit down.

The dog sped past the horse and felt sure he had captured the victory, with just a few more miles to go.

But as fate would have it, a beautiful lady French Poodle called out to Lucky.

"Hey Lucky, come and sit with me for a minute or two. You are so far ahead of the others. Come and spend a little time with me. I admire you so much. You are my hero," she

UNCLE YAH YAH: PART 2
21st Century Man of Wisdom

said. Lucky was mesmerized and in love at first sight.

Swifty the mouse zoomed past Lucky like a jet plane. The finish line was in sight. As Swifty got closer to the finish line, he could see Sloth Foot the turtle crossing the line in front of him.

Sloth was the winner, Swifty was second, and Lightning and Lucky were disqualified.

As Sloth Foot held high his reward, Swifty asked, "How did you get out in front of us? You were in last place starting out, I never saw you pass me."

"That is because you were asleep when I passed you. I never stopped running for anything, not even a drink of water," said the turtle.

A WINNER NEVER QUITS, AND A QUITTER NEVER WINS!

-End-

UNCLE YAH YAH: PART 2
21st Century Man of Wisdom

THE SQUIRREL AND THE RABBIT

The squirrel and the rabbit were the best of friends. They had enjoyed the greatest of fun and games all summer long. But as the leaves began to turn in color, the squirrel had less time to play tag and fool around. He began to busy himself with finding acorns and burying them.

The rabbit couldn't understand this abrupt change in the squirrel's behavior. "Hey squirrel, you gonna fool around with those acorns all day? Come on, I'll race you to the big oak tree. I want to have some fun," said the rabbit.

"I am not fooling around. I am working. I have got to find and bury some more acorns before I have time to play," said the squirrel, as a matter of fact.

UNCLE YAH YAH: PART 2
21st Century Man of Wisdom

The rabbit couldn't believe his ears. "No time for play, the squirrel must be losing his mind," he thought.

"I think you have a real problem, squirrel. How long have you had this compulsion to find and bury acorns? I know a doctor that can help you," the rabbit said with a great show of sympathy.

The squirrel said, "Hey man, I am not crazy. You are the one who is crazy if you think winter is not coming this year. And you are crazy if you think someone is going to bring you food. Have you put any food up for storage so you and your family can live through this winter?"

"No, I have not put up any food, but you can't talk to me like that," the rabbit said, puffed up with pride.

"Get mad if you want to, but I am telling you that all you have to do is think of how hard it was to survive last winter and you will get busy finding food for this winter," said the squirrel as he buried another acorn.

The rabbit said, "Yeah, right!" Then he hopped playfully off into the forest.

The squirrel called out:
"REMEMBER, IT IS BETTER TO HAVE IT AND NOT NEED IT, THAN TO NEED IT AND NOT HAVE IT!"
-End-

UNCLE YAH YAH: PART 2
21st Century Man of Wisdom

THE FIELD MOUSE AND THE CITY MOUSE

This winter Alawishes, the field mouse, lived in the country with his family. Alawishes hated the country. He wanted to live in the big city. His family begged him not to go, but he would not listen. He was obsessed with the bright lights and the fast life city folks lived.

Alawishes bought a Greyhound ticket, called his cousin in New York and asked him to meet him at the bus station.

Kool Joe, the city mouse, was there when Alawishes arrived. "Hey cousin Al, over here. Hurry up, man," Kool Joe, called out, peeking out from behind a post.

"Oh, there you are. How are you doing, cousin Kool Joe? And why are you standing

UNCLE YAH YAH: PART 2
21st Century Man of Wisdom

behind this post? Is anything wrong?" asked Alawishes.

"Be quiet. Look over there. See the drunken possum sitting on that bench?" whispered Joe.

"Yeah, what about him?" asked Al.

"That is our meal ticket. He is our mark. You stand right here while I make this sting," said Joe.

"What are you talking about? I don't understand," said Al.

"Man I thought you were ready for the city life, but you are really square. Look, that possum's got a wine bottle in his hand and he's asleep. He's got a gold ring, a watch, and I can see his wallet sticking out of his coat pocket. Man, this is a gift. This mark is made for us. I'm going to make my move. You stand right here, and if you see the police coming let me know," Kool said, as he eased over to the bench and sat next to the drunken possum.

Al was excited. He had just stepped off the bus and stuff was happening already. He didn't know what to think, so he thought it best to do as Kool Joe said. After all, Kool knew about these things.

Al saw Kool take the drunk's watch and ring and was reaching in the coat to take the wallet when the drunk jumped up, pulled out a badge and said, "I'm a police officer. You are under arrest!"

Kool pushed the officer aside and ran straight to Alawishes and gave him the watch and ring and said, "Stay here, I'll be back," as he ran off.

The undercover police officer grabbed Alawishes. By that time two back up cops had arrived on the scene.

"I got one of them. The other one got away," the decoy cop said.

Alawishes went to pieces. "Oh no, this is all a mistake. I didn't do nothing. I don't want to go to jail. Please, I've never done anything. It was my cousin Kool Joe, the city mouse. He took those things and gave them to me as he ran off. I just got here from the country. Please, let me go back home," poor Al sobbed.

"I know Kool Joe," said the back-up officer. "He's a penny ante thief. I can find him. I think this guy is telling the truth. Let's let him go."

The other officers agreed, but they gave poor Al, who was crying, a stern warning. They told him to go back home, and that if he ever came back to the city they would throw him in jail.

UNCLE YAH YAH: PART 2
21st Century Man of Wisdom

Al was on the next bus going back to the country. He had, had all he wanted of the city.

Every deed has a consequence, and you must endure that consequence. If you can't stand the consequence don't do the deed.

In other words:

IF YOU CAN'T STAND THE HEAT, STAY OUT OF THE KITCHEN. DON'T DO THE CRIME IF YOU CAN'T DO THE TIME.

-End-

UNCLE YAH YAH: PART 2
21st Century Man of Wisdom

SLICK THE RACCOON

Old Judge Fox sentenced Slick the Raccoon to thirty years to life imprisonment under the habitual criminal act.

All the hustlers, gamblers, thieves, and street folks from downtown felt it was a great travesty of justice, and that poor Slick was a good man. What a great lost. Slick's after hours joint would be closed now.

But Slick was not to be outdone. No sooner had he reached the prison he started planning his escape.

"Slick, do you know what you are doing?" said a fellow inmate, Chubby the bear, who was in for burglary. "These prison guards will shoot to kill if you try to get out of here."

Slick the Raccoon thought for a few seconds, and then he said, "I'd rather be killed trying to escape. At least I would die one time and be done with it. I think that is much better than dying a few times every day for the next thirty years."

Better to die once, than to live in terror everyday!

PERSECUTION IS WORST THAN SLAUGHTER.

-End-

UNCLE YAH YAH: PART 2
21st Century Man of Wisdom

THE CRANE AND THE BLACKBIRD

The Crane and the Blackbird were arguing as to how many teeth a horse has.

"I have been around horses all my life, and I'm telling you that horses have more than twenty teeth," said the Blackbird.

"No, no, no. I had some neighbors that were horses, and I even had a playmate who was a horse. He used to show me his teeth all the time, and I'm telling you that horses never have more than fifteen teeth," said the Crane, offering his rebuttal.

An owl, who was trying to take a nap, and finding it more and more difficult, due to the racket caused by the Crane and the Blackbird said, "Hey, will you guys knock it off! I'm

UNCLE YAH YAH: PART 2
21st Century Man of Wisdom

trying to get some sleep up here. And furthermore, if you really want to know how many teeth a horse has, go find one and count his teeth," said the owl, angrily ruffling his feathers as he shouted.

"It is bad enough," the owl continued, "to argue about what you don't know, and even worse to argue that which you do know."

The Blackbird and the Crane knew that the admonishment of the owl was true. Embarrassed and crestfallen, they said not another word, and flew off in different directions like two bats out of hell.

NEVER ARGUE!

-End-

UNCLE YAH YAH: PART 2
21st Century Man of Wisdom

THE WISE OLD MONK

A wise old Buddhist Monk was meditating under a boa tree, as was his habit at noon-time, when out of the shadows a King Cobra snuck right up in front of him.

"Open your eyes, holy man. I want to see the fear on your face before I sting you to death," the snake said.

The holy man slowly opened his eyes, and without changing the expression on his face, and using a calm voice, said, "Thank you King Cobra for waking me up before you struck. Now I can warn you and save your life. Just a while ago, one of your brother snakes snuck and bit me, only to have discovered that I am more poisonous than all the serpents in the world. Then the poor thing crawled off and died. There he is lying dead right over there," the holy man said.

As the King Cobra looked around to see his dead brother, the holy man, quick as a flash, grabbed a stick and hit the snake on the head. The blow was so hard it cracked the snake's skull.

But before the snake died he said, "You tricked me. You lied! There is no dead snake over there. You are a holy man, why did you lie?"

The holy man said, "YOU CAN'T MASTER TRUTH UNLESS YOU MASTER THE LIE ALSO."

The snake died and the holy man whispered, "Buddha be praised," as he closed his eyes again to meditate.

-End-

UNCLE YAH YAH: PART 2
21st Century Man of Wisdom

THE SPIDER

It was a bright and early morning, which found Robin Redbreast living up to his reputation of being an early bird.

"Chasing worms can be quite tiring," the robin thought as he flew to a window ledge.

The Robin noticed a little spider on the other side of the windowpane. It looked like the spider was trying to climb to the top of the glass, but every time he got close to the top, down he'd slide again.

"Hey in there," said the robin as he tapped his beak to get the spider's attention.

"Young man, I know you're sour and angry about not making it to the top after repeated efforts, but you should know when to accept defeat. Isn't it obvious that you can't get up there? You might as well face it," sermonized

UNCLE YAH YAH: PART 2
21st Century Man of Wisdom

the Robin.

The spider leaped into action. Again, he was climbing as fast as his legs would carry him. Up he went until he made it all the way to the top of the window. The spider was sporting a big smile as he called out to the robin.

"Sir, I'm not at all angry or sour. THERE IS NO SUCH THING AS CAN'T. ANYTHING YOU CONCEIVE, YOU CAN BRING ABOUT! IF YOU DONT SUCCEED AT FIRST, YOU TRY AGAIN. ALSO, YOU CAN BELIEVE ME WHEN I TELL YOU, DEFEAT IS ONLY BITTER WHEN YOU SWALLOW IT."

The robin couldn't think of anything to say, so he flew off to chase some more worms.

-End-

UNCLE YAH YAH: PART 2
21st Century Man of Wisdom

NOAH

It was just a few weeks after the great flood, and Noah, the prophet of God, was still a little shaky. His escape was narrow to say the least. As he thought about the anger of the Lord, against the sinful transgressions of those He had drowned, Noah wondered if ever man would do the same thing again.

Noah decided to satisfy his curiosity by taking a brief look into the future of man. He placed a crystal ball on the table and took a peek.

There it was; he saw it. The year was 1988. Noah was suddenly in Harlem on Lenox Avenue in New York, New York. He was standing in front of an appliance store, where a television set was broadcasting the news in the window.

UNCLE YAH YAH: PART 2
21st Century Man of Wisdom

All about him, Noah saw addiction, partying, adultery, and all manner of foul things. The TV news reporter had given more shocking revelations. "Bulletin, this just in:

*Africa reports five million new cases of the deadly AIDS infection. The disease, common among homosexuals, has crossed over to the heterosexual population. It is expected to reach the one billion mark by 1993, if no preventive cure is discovered.

*Iraq has admitted to bombing non-combatants (civilians) with poison gas, which killed 275,000, hospitalizing 100,000. Iraq is being charged with war crimes by the United Nations.

*Two children, ages ten and eleven, have been arrested for being the local kingpins of a cocaine and prostitution ring in Newark, New Jersey. An hour after their arraignment, in Judge Cook's courtroom, a one million dollar bail was posted and they both were released.

*Acid rain and other pollutants have destroyed one-third of the fish and waterways, one-third of the forest and animal habitats, and the quality of air we breathe is diminishing faster than expected. This comes from the scientists of Canada and America, who have just completed a study at the Ecological Center in Washington, D.C."

Noah could not stand to watch anymore. He quickly put his crystal ball back in its box.

"O Lord," Noah lamented with tears streaming down his black cheeks, "Is there any hope for mankind? To be sure, he is the most foolish of all Your creation. Dear Lord, they are going straight back to the same old wicked and sinful behavior, which provoked your anger and brought the flood in the first place."

God said unto Noah, "Remember: THE MORE THINGS CHANGE THE MORE THEY REMAIN THE SAME. They don't realize that I will bring the Fire Next Time!"

-End-

WISDOM

Part Two

UNCLE YAH YAH: PART 2
21st Century Man of Wisdom

UNCLE YAH YAH: PART 2
21st Century Man of Wisdom

Women are God's original gift to man.
***
Loving makes you lovable.
***
You are what you love.
***
Difficulty and Ease are two criminals, lock them up and live at peace.
***
Courage is not the friend of Hope or Fear.
***
The loving kiss of a goddess makes you immortal.
***
Feed God's sheep and God will feed you.
***
Feed the masses and the masses will become your kingdom.
***
Life is purpose and goals. Death is doing nothing and going nowhere.
***
Sincerity is the express train of the soul; it takes you nonstop to your destination.
***
Peace is like the fabled tar baby, once you got your hands on it, you can't turn it loose.

UNCLE YAH YAH: PART 2
21st Century Man of Wisdom

***

Give charity to self before giving to others.

***

It is the hands of women which fashion civilization.

***

Skill is always in demand.

***

Love the maker, not that which is made.

***

A man with four wives, in love and unity of God, is in heaven on earth. A man with one wife, who lies, nags and is rebellious, can experience no greater hell.

***

He who knows peace, keeps the peace.

***

Ignorance is the second greatest power in the universe.

***

Speak right and do right.

***

Death of the body is temporary. Death of the soul is forever.

***

If you want to unite the spirit, unite the blood.

***

UNCLE YAH YAH: PART 2
21st Century Man of Wisdom

Does God dance? Of course he does!

***

If you want your children to love you, then you must love your women.

***

When the secret of the spirituality of sexuality is made known, the churches and the preachers will be cast into the fiery pit and destroyed.

***

The greater the Hope, the greater the Fear.

***

Live for today. Yesterday is gone and tomorrow hasn't got here yet.

***

To restore the dead means to teach the light of truth to the ignorant.

***

Every wise man is a child.

***

Reason is the vehicle. Passion is the driver.

***

Suspicion in most cases is just a reflection of your fears.

***

War protects peace.

***

UNCLE YAH YAH: PART 2
21st Century Man of Wisdom

The more things change the more they remain the same.

***

To save your life you must be ready, at a moment's notice, to give your life.

***

Custom is the real slave master.

***

Show me a cruel oppressor and I'll show you a coward.

***

Reality is created by God. Imagination is created by man.

***

God is above praise or blame.

***

Our greatest enemies are ignorance, anger, lust, and indifference.

***

No peace, no happiness. Can't have one without the other.

***

A nation stays here, or leaves here, according to what it eats mentally and physically.
You are what you eat.

***

Your body is the house of God, if you are

anything like me, then God's temple is in need of much repair.

***

Trust no one but God.

***

What affects the heavens above, affects the earth below.

***

Your ego is nothing but a dream.

***

You can't hold your children to the past, but you can follow them into the future.

***

The haves and the have-nots are natural enemies.

***

God makes laws for man. Man does not make laws for God.

***

Everything that happens on this planet affects all of us directly or indirectly.

***

Look for the beauty in everything and you'll never get old.

***

You need big ears to hear self-criticism.

***

Moderation is the key.

UNCLE YAH YAH: PART 2
21st Century Man of Wisdom

***

One not affected by bliss or misery has everything because he belongs to nothing.

***

Group prayer creates a group mind.

***

Time exists for those in a hurry.

***

Life offers no perpetration.

***

What you think life is, is how it is for you.

***

You are possessed by God or the devil. It's your choice.

***

Your duty to God is the only reality.

***

God is not subject to anything or anybody.

***

Teachers are closest to God.

***

The truly wise follow the Laws of God.

***

The ignorant can't see God.

***

Never look back in anger or forward in fear, but look around in awareness.

***

UNCLE YAH YAH: PART 2
21st Century Man of Wisdom

Why are you here?

***

Life continues, things understood before are still understood today.

***

Learn to control yourself before trying to control others.

***

Which is better, to be cared for, or to care for self?

***

Everything comes in pairs.

***

A braggart is an obsessed person.

***

When the one great scorer comes to put His mark besides your name, He judges not if you won or lost, but the way you played the game.
-Winton Rice

***

To revolt, is the nature in which mankind is created. He responds to pressure. Historically, the greater the tyrannical oppression, the greater the revolt.

***

Communism and capitalism are the heads and tails of the same dime.

***

UNCLE YAH YAH: PART 2
21st Century Man of Wisdom

You are truly wise when you can smile the same smile when you lose, that you smile when you win.

***

Fame, honor, and disaster are cultural illusions.

***

The dirty, stinking, and foul mouth of the gossiper attracts flies and fools.

***

He who seeks the company of the wise, himself is wise. Association breeds similarity.

***

Flattery will kill you quicker than pure poison.

***

Your ears must grow larger than those of the jackass if you want to hear self-criticism.

***

Wherever pride goes shame follows.

***

Give good advice to the wise, and he will love you; advise the fool and he will hate you.

***

Your good deeds go with you to and beyond the grave.

***

UNCLE YAH YAH: PART 2
21st Century Man of Wisdom

What you don't use you lose.
***

How you see it is how it is for you. What you see is what you get.
***

A loose woman is like a gold tooth in the mouth of a pig.
***

Trust nobody but God.
***

When gossip comes, love and unity goes.
***

If it is not worth fighting for it is not worth having.
***

The rougher the trial the tougher you become.
***

If the trial doesn't kill you it makes you strong.
***

Your money makes no impression on God.
***

The will of man cannot be captured or restrained.
***

Next to God, women are all that are worshipful.

UNCLE YAH YAH: PART 2
21st Century Man of Wisdom

***

Stand ready to lose all that you have and be attached to nothing, because the same way you got that you can get some more.

***

Remain calm, even in the face of the greatest difficulties.

***

All things change. Nothing remains the same except God and Truth.

***

Nothing is more hateful than the sound of arrogant boasting and the braying of donkeys.

***

Hard times do purify.

***

There is nothing more valuable, or beautiful, than a good woman.

Your tomorrow is your children, your yesterdays your parents. All you have is today!

***

Live everyday as if it were your last, because it is! Life does not walk in the same footsteps twice. We only get one ticket for one ride on the merry-go-round called life.

***

Fear and ignorance are like two poisonous

snakes whose sting paralyzes and blinds you.

***

Oppression, like the scorpion, will sting itself to death once surrounded by the flames of liberation.

***

The four most important things in life are: What you know, what you intend to do, prayer, and your woman.

***

The greatest occupation is the uplifting of humanity.

***

Love is the greatest power.

***

You are truly a master builder when you can build the temple using human blocks.

***

Nothing comes to a sleeper but a dream.

***

A hard head makes a soft behind.

***

The real slave masters are customs and traditions.

***

The better the government, the fewer its prisons.

***

UNCLE YAH YAH: PART 2
21st Century Man of Wisdom

The longest war is self-control.

***

Equality is a myth. There will always be classes of men.

***

"Ultimately, Love is God, and Being to Being is the Communion."
- Lao Tzu

***

A good woman is paradise found.

***

True love brings out the poet in you.

***

All great truths were first stomped under foot.

***

Wages should be paid to the wife and mother for her work.

***

Power doesn't corrupt man; it is man that corrupts power.

***

Freedom is like self-discipline, only a few have it.

***

This is a nation whose women and girls are kept under house arrest.

***

UNCLE YAH YAH: PART 2
21st Century Man of Wisdom

Their hatred of me is proof that I'm telling the truth. Now I understand Jesus saying, "Love your enemy."

***

Don't fear death. It is the best thing that can happen to a lot of folks I know.

***

Strengthen your soul and all things are given to you.

***

I am poor, penniless, and poverty-stricken-proof that my duty is to God and me only.

***

God doesn't allow evil to touch a good man.

***

Popular belief is that you are innocent until proven guilty, but I say you are insane until proven sane.

***

Love and care for your parents.

***

Women love only men they can worship.

***

All children are in danger of being shackled to the past.

***

"Nationalism is an infantile disease. It is

UNCLE YAH YAH: PART 2
21st Century Man of Wisdom

the measles of mankind."
—Albert Einstein, Scientist.

***

Fear keeps man a slave. God hates cowards.

***

Parents, your children owe you nothing; they filled your life with meaning and provided never a dull moment.

***

"There is no use arguing about polygamy, it must be taken as defacto. It exists everywhere, and the only question is how it shall be regulated. We all live, at any rate for a time and most of us always, in polygamy. And so, since every man needs many women, there is nothing fairer than to allow him, nay, to make it incumbent upon him, to provide for many women. This will reduce woman to her true and natural position as a subordinate being; and the lady (that monster of European civilization and Teutonic-Christian stupidity) evil will disappear from the world, leaving only women, but no more unhappy women, of which Europe is full of."
—Arthur Schopenhauer, German Philosopher (1788-1860)

***

UNCLE YAH YAH: PART 2
21st Century Man of Wisdom

The first thing created was sex.

***

One man's opinion is his religion; another man's religion is his opium.

***

Wisdom submits only to greater wisdom.

***

"There are no illegitimate children, only illegitimate parents."
— U.S District Court Judge Leon R. Yankwich

***

Wherever you find a wise man, there you find a king.

***

There has been no greater blessing than sex,
nor has there been anything causing more trouble or sin.

***

Woman is made from man and is ever in oneness with him.

***

Don't lie! Your word is all you have.

***

Holy sexual union brings spirit and flesh together. The union of spirit and flesh brings God into His temple, which is your heart.

UNCLE YAH YAH: PART 2
21st Century Man of Wisdom

***

There can be no greater hell than a bad woman.

***

Nothing delights the heart of man more than a young and beautiful woman.

***

Deny a man sexual expression and you create a demon or a saint.

***

Great civilizations depend on great women.

***

Hey, Big Incorporations just bought the government.

What are we going to do now?

***

Woe to the nation of dogs, which does not protect, cherish, honor, and respect its women.

***

The difference in a real man of God and the imposter is that the man of God has the power to turn human waste into gold. The imposter's waste stays waste.

***

The wise man is like the ocean. He must be capable of receiving the polluted streams of humanity without becoming polluted himself.

UNCLE YAH YAH: PART 2
21st Century Man of Wisdom

He purifies the unclean streams and sends them back clean, and as a healing for humanity.

***

When you think you are running from death, you are actually running to meet it. When you run to meet death, it runs from you.

***

Your boasting reveals the things in life you are helplessly chained to, obsessed with, and attached to.

***

"Now I do not believe the Almighty ever intended the Negro to be the equal of the white man. If He did, He has been a long time demonstrating the fact."
—Stephen A. Douglas, American Statesman (1813-1861).

***

Man can't be any better than the God he worships. Woman can't be any better than her man; and civilization can be no better than its women.

***

The end of a civilization can be measured by the height of the hemline of its women's dresses.

***

UNCLE YAH YAH: PART 2
21st Century Man of Wisdom

Everything depends on balance and skill.

***

The greater the pride, the harder you must fight to keep your pride from being hurt. That is a sick pastime. Better to give up pride, relax and enjoy life.

***

Nothing is more spirit lifting then meeting your fellow man on the level, and parting on the square and in peace.

***

The torment of defeat is only bitter when you swallow it.

***

Liberty depends on the freedom of the press.

***

To fight against slavery is obedience to God.

***

One person's loss is another person's gain.

***

Inferiority is just a fast trip to superiority.

***

There is a time for everything. Be wise; learn to tell time.

***

UNCLE YAH YAH: PART 2
21st Century Man of Wisdom

Stagnation, poor health, and disinterest are the offspring of old age.

***

Complain and no one listens, but offer compliments and you get an audience.

***

We lie only when we are afraid of the truth.

***

Life depends on the illumination of ideals.

***

"This would be the best of all possible worlds, if there was no religion in it."
—John Adams, second President U.S. (1735-1826)

***

If you can read, write, and think, you are equal to every man.

***

If ignorance were a physical monster, I would track it down and kill it.

***

When traditions and customs get in the way of progress, assassinate them.

***

Concentrate long enough on a thing, and eventually it becomes reality.

***

When you are not attached to anything, all

UNCLE YAH YAH: PART 2
21st Century Man of Wisdom

things are available to you.

***

Anything your mind can conceive, your hands can create.

***

You have two voices. One is good and one is bad. One is God and one is the devil.

***

Your future is custom made by the way your actions are today.

***

If we are the exact reproductions of Adam and Eve, then reincarnation is real.

***

You join the ranks of the immortals once you recognize God.

***

The knowledge that makes you know God, also makes you live forever.

***

Good deeds destroy evil.

***

The theater is a crack-dealer, too.

***

Give me this new generation today, and I'll give you the stars of tomorrow.

***

Flowery phrases and sweet sounding words

UNCLE YAH YAH: PART 2
21st Century Man of Wisdom

butter no biscuits. You must activate it by the work you do. Act like it and you'll be it!

***

The Truth is the domain of God; therefore, any truth spoken by anyone else is plagiarism.

***

There are two sides to every man: Emotional and realistic, right-side and left-side, male and female.

***

"Love takes time. It needs a history of giving and receiving, laughing and crying. Love never promises with instant gratification, only ultimate fulfillment. Love means believing in someone, in something. It supposes a willingness to struggle, to work, to suffer and to rejoice."

—Barb Upham

***

Actions speak louder than prayer.

***

When you walk with God you can do no wrong, nor can wrong do anything to you.

***

Live in this world, but not attached to it; like the lotus flower lives in the water,
   but is untouched by it.

***

UNCLE YAH YAH: PART 2
21st Century Man of Wisdom

Like a blade of grass pushing its way up through concrete, so will love always find a way.

***

First get wisdom then get money, or get money and then get wisdom,

but you must have both to have complete peace.

***

If you have no reason to live, then you are already in the grave.

***

Mental chains of slavery are just as destructive as physical chains.

***

Theory and doctrine have no authority over the knowledge of God.

***

Prayer is the fastest route to greatness.

***

Nothing to it but to do it!

***

Down doesn't mean out.

***

National Elections are the antidote to revolution.

***

UNCLE YAH YAH: PART 2
21st Century Man of Wisdom

There is always someone better on the way up.

***

Being male doesn't make you a man.

***

Anyone who allows the abuse of women is a scumbag and a coward!

***

UNCLE YAH YAH: PART 2
21st Century Man of Wisdom

FOOTPRINTS

One night a man had a dream. He dreamt he was walking along the beach with the Lord. Across the sky flashed scenes from his life. For each scene he noticed two sets of footprints in the sand, one belonging to him, and the other to the Lord.

When the last scene of his life flashed before him, he looked back at the footprints in the sand. He noticed that many times, along the path of his life, there was only one set of footprints. He also noticed that it happened at the very lowest and saddest times in his life.

This really bothered him and he questioned the Lord about it. "Lord, you said that once I decided to follow You, You would walk with me all the way. But I have noticed that during the most troublesome times in my life, there is only one set of footprints. I don't understand why, when I needed you most, you would leave me.

The Lord replied, "My precious child, I love you and I would never leave you. During your times of trials and suffering, when you see only one set of footprints, it was then that I was carrying you."

—Author Unknown

***

UNCLE YAH YAH: PART 2
21st Century Man of Wisdom

YAH YAH'S DREAM

WHILE FASTING I RECEIVED THE ORDER TO write something especially for my beloved disciples. I do not expect too many of you will be admitted to the glory of what I am about to say; not that I am closing you out, no, not at all. I am putting it all right before your eyes. It is for you regardless of how long it takes for you to receive and act upon it.

History teaches that most people wake up to the Truth by degrees. Only a few are blessed to wake up to everything at once. Only Gods and Prophets do that.

So read, listen to your heart, and learn all about yourself.

There is the positive and negative, and the power and force that is between these extremes. Of course, some of you wise guys will say, "Oh, but there are many more dimensions. A fourth, fifth, sixth and seventh. Also, there is the same number of worlds and universes in every one dimension."

Yes, you are right, but you don't have my job. I have to make it plain; I have to let them know. So why belabor the fact that the universe is unlimited. We can add zeros from now until doomsday, and still not even begin to know all the heavens.

So, being that we are a true microcosm of creation, then all we really need to do is study here and now. My job is to get you into what's happening now!

Let us bring the Supreme Being down to earth. Let us deal with the facts of this generation. Think of the Lord being here now, and He is waging a campaign against the existing opposing forces.

We are the Lord's agents. He has given us the germination of Truth. We must infect as many as we can with this Truth. You should be constantly introducing this Truth to people you meet. Tell them of your Teacher, the Source of your wisdom. The more people we infect with this knowledge, the faster we will have power over this world to create a better world of Truth and Justice for us all.

UNCLE YAH YAH: PART 2
21st Century Man of Wisdom

The Real people will wake up upon hearing this Truth. Many will hear it and just carry it. So don't try to figure out who you should, or should not preach to. Every day you should be teaching the Truth. They will join us when they know. It is you, disciples, who are obligated to do this work. Your God gave you the wisdom that you are now famous for. Our Lord chose you to be the first to receive these New Revelations. You must now speak out in plain words that God is a man and the devil is man, and that we must teach and raise more angels for God.

If your Lord is living in heavenly luxury, peaceful and contented, and His wives, children, and family are perfectly happy with His Kingship and the guidance of His words—then you have no excuse for not having your own kingdom, or your own heaven. Your Lord is the living proof. It is a fact all over the universe that if you follow in the footsteps of the One you recognize as your Lord, Leader and Teacher, then whatever He has accomplished you too must accomplish.

His Ways are taught to you by your Lord, and then He shows you how to practice the rules of success. You can't go wrong. You know God, you see God, you follow God, you

UNCLE YAH YAH: PART 2
21st Century Man of Wisdom

become God!

His ways deliver us from evil, sickness, and death. You must do as God does. He is the Greatest Teacher. Were it not for Him being on His job of teaching, we would not be here now. He was not afraid or ashamed to tell the Truth. The Lord will preach every chance He gets.

We are all gods and children of the Most High. Take those human bricks and start building your kingdom in the image of God's Kingdom. Want what the Lord wants. Watch His Life and imitate the life of your Lord. Rule your world like God Rules His—with the Divine Law He gave you. Never disobey God, and never help the devil keep the people of God deaf, dumb, and blind.

Feed the sheep and the Lord will feed you. Give credit to whom credit is due.

Ralph Waldo Emerson (1803-1882), a philosopher, gave us this great advice: "O my brothers, God exists. There is a Soul at the center of nature and over the will of every man, so that none of us wrong the universe. The simplest person, who in his integrity worships God, becomes God. If a man is just at heart, then in so far is he God; the safety of God, the immortality of God, the Majesty of

UNCLE YAH YAH: PART 2
21st Century Man of Wisdom

God, do enter into that man with Justice.

And now my brothers, you will ask, what in these depending days can be done by us? Wherever a man comes, there comes revolution. The old is for the slaves. When a man comes, all books are legible, all things transparent, all religions are forms.

Yourself, a newborn lord of the Holy Ghost, cast behind you all conformity, and acquaint men at firsthand with Deity, but live with the privilege of the immeasurable Mind.

The hour of that choice is the crisis of your history. Be content with a little light, so it be your own. Explore and explore. Make yourself necessary to the world and mankind will give you bread."

Thank you brother Waldo for that jewel of wisdom. Take your knowledge, wisdom, and understanding and get great wealth. Gather your people and love, bless, and protect them as God has done by you. Do God's Will always, that He may manifest His Holy Ghost in you. You are all God's.

Go your way. The earth is yours and all that is in it. Praise the Lord, the Most High, and go in Peace.

UNCLE YAH YAH: PART 2
21st Century Man of Wisdom

UFO REPORT

I HADN'T REALIZED I'D READ THE WHOLE book. As I closed it and looked around the room, everyone was silent. I let the manuscript rest in my lap. No one said a word. The room was deathly quiet, like the aftermath of an atomic blast. The only sound was the electrical storm generated by the billions of thought waves bouncing off the walls of our individual brains. We all sat there hanging in space; it was only for a few moments, but it seemed like an eternity. We were awestruck, bombed-out, and drunk from so much wisdom.

I began to have questioning thoughts: What are you doing with your life? Who are you, Rudy? Is having a job, some food, and a roof over your head all that there is to life?

UNCLE YAH YAH: PART 2
21st Century Man of Wisdom

No, that's not what I want, I thought. Living from day to day, just to eat and sleep, until I die is a life wasted. I want to do something positive. I want to make my mark for future generations to see. I want to raise myself up to be a leader of my family, my clan, my tribe, and my nation. I want to be like Uncle Yah Yah, or better still, I will join him in his work to uplift humanity. Yeah, that's right! I can make Uncle Yah Yah's work my mission in life. I'm not going back home; I will stay right here, I thought to myself and meant it!

I broke the silence. "Hey, Brother-in-law Dear, can I get a job here at Paradise?"

Brother-in-law Dear looked puzzled. He said, "I thought you were going back home after your vacation?"

"No, I just made my mind up. I'm staying," I answered.

"Do you want to work in the dining room as a waiter? If so, you can have my job. I'm sure I can fix it up with Mrs. Walters."

"What about you?"

"Oh, Sue and I are leaving for Germany this week. Uncle Yah Yah wants us to become doctors. We are going to study at the Frankfort School of Medicine. Both of our jobs are

UNCLE YAH YAH: PART 2
21st Century Man of Wisdom

available."

"Well, waiting tables is fine with me. All that really matters is that I'll be here."

"Right-on, Rudy," Freda said with a big smile and a clinched fist raised high in salute. "Uncle Yah Yah said if you decided to stay he would consider putting you on the Grand Tour, because you have the spirit of a great teacher if you submit to it."

"What's the Grand Tour?" I asked.

"It's being sent to be taught by twelve of Uncle Yah Yah's best masters. Each one has a different lesson to teach you," Freda responded.

"Were any of you ever on the Grand Tour?" I asked.

Brother-in-law Dear answered, "No, but we all wish we could've been chosen."

"Well, what qualifies one to be chosen?" I asked.

"I don't know. Uncle Yah Yah is the only one to make that choice," Brother-in-law Dear said.

Then Sue spoke up. "I was told that only the spiritually gifted are chosen to be preachers."

"Yeah, that's right," Freda agreed.

Everyone got quiet again and I began to

UNCLE YAH YAH: PART 2
21st Century Man of Wisdom

think about what all this Grand Tour stuff could mean. Freda said, "Isn't Uncle Yah Yah something else?"

We all said our amen to that.

"I've lived with him for three years and he still holds me spellbound whenever I hear him speak, or I read something he has written. Just when I think I've heard all he has to say, he comes up with something new. He is like an ever-flowing stream. I am really going to hate to leave," Freda said.

"Where are you going, Freda?" I asked.

"I'm going home. Work has started on my school. They broke ground a few days ago. It's my dream come true, so you know I've got to be there," she said with an air of pride.

"That's good, Freda, I'm happy for you. We all are, I'm sure," I told her.

"Guess who will be taking my job at Uncle Yah Yah's house?" Freda asked.

"Who?" I asked in anticipation.

"Dottie," she said, pointing a finger toward Dottie sitting next to her.

"Hey, well go ahead with your bad self, Dottie. You have really moved up in the world," I teased.

"Yeah, I'm still not used to being around Uncle Yah Yah yet. I keep thinking that he's

UNCLE YAH YAH: PART 2
21st Century Man of Wisdom

just too wise to be ordinary, but I'm fast learning that he's just like his teachings, plain and simple, not complicated. Like what he said about holy sexual union. Remember? He quoted Lao Tzu's The Tao Te Ching, "That ultimately love is God, and being to being is the communion." Also, the phrase, 'The kingdom of God is within you,' makes all the pieces fit. That is the key to the basic nature of every man," she said.

Dottie would have gone on all night, but Brother-in-law Dear wanted to join her trend of thought. He cut in and said, "Uncle Yah Yah said God is true Love and Love is the greatest power in the universe. Sex is the simplest act, but the most important to a perfect life. There are two times when man can become one with God—in death and in sex!"

Dottie and Brother-in-law Dear continued to converse about the simplicity of Uncle Yah Yah and his teachings. I was listening with one ear and trying to hear myself think with the other ear. My thoughts kept going back to the Grand Tour. When I got the chance to squeeze a word in I asked, "Are the Twelve Masters here in Paradise Garden?"

"No, they are all over the country and all over the world for that matter. They never stay

UNCLE YAH YAH: PART 2
21st Century Man of Wisdom

in one place too long. You are sent to them one at a time, to wherever he or she may be," Freda said.

"Oh, there are women masters, too?" I asked.

"Yeah, there are three I believe. Is that right?" Freda asked Brother-in-law Dear.

"Yes, there are three, not counting Aunt Willie Mae," he said as he stood up and stretched. Then he said, "I think we'd better be going, Sue. It's getting late."

Sue got to her feet and said, "Well, we have to go." She took her husband's hand and they left as we wished them a good night.

"How did you like those animal stories, Rudy?" Dottie asked.

"Wonderful! I thought all of them were real good. Maybe even better than the first manuscript. I liked all of it," I said, as I started to drift off into thought again. The Grand Tour, ain't that something. Am I really going to be a preacher? My thoughts raced on and on.

I heard Freda say, "Well Dottie, I guess we'd better go. Rudy has fallen asleep on us."

Dottie said, "Yeah, just look at him sitting there nodding."

"I'm not sleep. I was just thinking," I

UNCLE YAH YAH: PART 2
21st Century Man of Wisdom

protested.

"Yeah, right," Freda said, "with your eyes closed, huh?"

"Uncle Yah Yah said, 'Every closed eye ain't sleep'," I said in retort. We all had a good laugh at that one.

"Yeah, but we do have to go. It's late and Aunt Willie Mae is probably wondering what happened to us," Freda said. She reached for her pocketbook lying on the bed. Then Dottie stood up and began to adjust her dress.

"Hey, wait a minute," I said. "I thought you were going to spend the night. What's going on here?" I tried my wounded puppy look out on them—it didn't work.

"Sorry, but we have to go," Freda said.

"So both of you are leaving? Oh man, this is killing my ego. What about you, Dottie? Ain't you in my debt?" I asked, as I pretended to be looking for a book of recorded debts.

"There is no hurry. I'll see you tomorrow," Dottie said like a tenant holding out on the rent.

They both said good night and let themselves out the door. I don't know why I didn't escort them to their quarters, or at least to the door. I just sat there like a kid who was just denied candy and watched them leave.

UNCLE YAH YAH: PART 2
21st Century Man of Wisdom

I was tired. It had been a busy night. My brain and my body needed rest. The next thing I knew my chin fell to my chest, but I was still lucid enough to prompt myself to get up, lock the door, and go to bed.

Sometime later, I opened my eyes and saw that I had Uncle Yah Yah's manuscript in my hand. I reached for the large manila envelope on the night table. In lifting it, a white business envelope fell on the bed. I picked it up and noticed it was open and had UFO REPORT typed across the front. There were three typed pages inside, so I began to read.

THIS IS THE RECORD OF THE NIGHT AN UNIDENTIFIED FLYING OBJECT VISITED ME. It was August 17, 1973, at 10:00 P.M. I was on the thirty-first day of my fast. The night was very calm and the sky was full of stars. I had been meditating on the front porch of my cabin for about half an hour when the spaceship made its appearance. Suddenly, I heard a voice whisper my name. As I opened my eyes to investigate, it was then that I received the shock of my life.

About twenty feet in the air, suspended above me, was what looked like a flying saucer. It was black and had red and green lights around the base of it. It was not a perfect circle. It was egg-shaped and had what looked like three half balls on its underside.

It made a soft humming sound and I felt something like restraint, but peaceful, like a baby held in the arms of its mother. I saw no one, only the ship hovering over my head; but someone was communicating with me telepathically.

The voice said, "Be at peace, Yah Yah. We have come to give you good news to pass on to mankind—the Thirteen Greatest Rules. These rules will prepare this world's civilization to meet and communicate with us in the starry heavens, and especially the seven inhabited planets, which are your neighbors.

In the beginning we delivered every earth-man unto Satan that you could learn to lie, murder, steal, sin in every way, and even to blaspheme the Supreme Being. We cast you into the bowels of hell, so that the flames of hell would burn away your wickedness, and purify your soul for the acceptance of righteousness. So be it! That you would learn godliness and a True Love of the Laws of the Supreme Being. So you would value Divine Laws more than silver and gold.

You are now perfect having the spirit of Satan in the flesh and the spirit of the Living

UNCLE YAH YAH: PART 2
21st Century Man of Wisdom

God in the flesh. Let your heart germinate Truth, keep the faith in right actions, charity, sobriety, and holiness. Great has been the controversy and mystery of the Supreme man living in God and God living in you.

Be not deceived, we are closer to you than the pumping of your heart. Call on us. We will never fail to answer. Yes, even before you ask, it shall be given.

Meditate on these divine exhortations, for in these words you will find the rites of passage through the golden gates of the universe, and the intercession to the Holy Temple. The key to tune-in is within you. For He is the One True and Living God Who exists in us all. Let the Lord be praised!

These are the Thirteen Greatest Rules. Write these down and teach them so this planet can save itself from self-destruction. This is the last chance given to them to establish peace on earth. Let the Lord be praised!

UNCLE YAH YAH: PART 2
21st Century Man of Wisdom

THE THIRTEEN GREATEST RULES

1. The Greatest Thought: Is the Supreme Being

2. The Greatest Power: Is Love

3. The Greatest Weakness: Is lack of Faith

4. The Greatest Certainty: Is Change

5. The Greatest Sickness: Is Fear

6. The Greatest Danger: Is Ignorance

7. The Greatest Force: Is Truth

8. The Greatest Time: Is Now

9. The Greatest Good: Is Peace

10. The Greatest Blessing: Is understanding, health, and patience

11. The Greatest Enemy: Is pride, egoism, and hate

12. The Greatest Victory: Is self-control

13. The Greatest Sin: Is lying

UNCLE YAH YAH: PART 2
21st Century Man of Wisdom

Take these rules and feed them to all the human family of the earth. These rules will bring you in line with us and will make you King of kings and Lord of lords.

The stars of heaven will guide and protect you like nursing mothers and fathers. Your earth will become a garden of civilized bliss. You will know no sickness or death. You will live in happiness forever. Let the Lord be praised!"

Amen.

The ship moved off and up like a fast moving elevator, and was out of sight in less than three seconds. I rushed inside the cabin and wrote this report.

***

My brain was knocked into total disorientation. I didn't know if I was dreaming all this with my eyes wide opened, or if this incredible report was real.

My mind was too tired to figure it out. I just didn't have the strength to think another thought. I put the report back into the envelope, rested my head on the back of the chair, and closed my eyes. My mind made one last attempt to seduce me. What is this Grand Tour and is this UFO Report real? "Don't even try it," I said to my brain. "I'm just too tired to think any more."

Right then it came upon me, the sweet mercy of sleep, comforting and covering me like the little red security blanket of Linus and Snoopy in the Peanuts comic strip. But not even in my dreams could I escape what was apparently to be my destiny.

In my dream, I was standing on the speaker's platform looking into the faces of thousands of attentive listeners. My voice was loud and had a mystic power that enthralled my dream audience.

"You are not ordinary people," I intoned. "You are supermen and superwomen. If you have the Will and the discipline, you can accomplish anything. You can be a good for nothing, or you can be great.

"It is your choice. You can will into existence whatever you desire, and with the power of stick-to-it-iveness, what you desire you must become. That is the law of the universe.

"Everything in the material world is the result of someone's creative thoughts. The mental world is real. The material world only appears to be real. First comes the word, or the articulation of the idea, then the eyes and ears bear witness to it. Then the hands fashion the

UNCLE YAH YAH: PART 2
21st Century Man of Wisdom

image into existence, or reality. All matter is conscious and all consciousness exists in matter.

"And last, but not least, learn to control your emotions. If you don't control yourself, you will be controlled. You must be calm in order to hear your creative inner voice. Life's ups and downs are like cooking food. If it doesn't turn out right just hold your nose until the stench passes.

"Man knows only what he sees and sees only what he knows. Wisdom is knowing what time it is. There is a time and a season for everything. When a thing is on time it is beautiful. When it is out of time it is ugly. Timing is true wisdom. Truth in its time is greater than an atomic bomb.

"All things are possible to you. As in God, so in man. This is no joke. You can create what you Will. Your happiness or your suffering is the consequence of your own deeds. You are what you think you are. Flying carpets are no joke. This is for real."

My dream audience was on their feet and cheering. I continued, "I am humbled by your generous applause, but we must remember that this inspirational message comes from Uncle Yah Yah. It is he who is constantly searching

UNCLE YAH YAH: PART 2
21st Century Man of Wisdom

the natural world, and researching scriptural history, to bring us Divine Guidance in the way of positive thinking.

"You and I are truly fortunate to have this twenty-first century Wise-Man among us. It is the teachings of Uncle Yah Yah that gives us one last chance to make ourselves a better people, and to build a better world.

"Those of us who have benefited from this knowledge must now help Uncle Yah Yah in whatever way we can. Those of us who know Truth must help Uncle Yah Yah spread this Truth. We must teach this Truth to the young and the old, in the East and the West, and in the North as well as the South.

We must help Uncle Yah Yah shout it out from the alleyways of skid row to the mansions of Beverly Hills. We must help Uncle Yah Yah shout it out in the halls of government, and all the way to the darkest dungeons in the prison houses of this country. Don't ever forget that this is our last chance. We must help Uncle Yah Yah."

Again, my dream audience rose to their feet with thunderous applause. My spirit was lifted higher and higher until I found myself among the clouds. I was sitting on a flying carpet with Uncle Yah Yah facing me. A big crystal ball rested on a stand between us. Uncle Yah Yah was pointing to the crystal. I looked into it and saw a beautiful monarch butterfly.

Uncle Yah Yah said, "The butterfly is a symbol of the power of the universe and the spirit of man. All things are developing and in a state of change. The butterfly starts his life as a larvae. It then develops into a caterpillar. It then spins a cocoon and finally emerges as a butterfly.

"Man too starts his spiritual life hardly aware of anything but himself. Between adolescence and maturity man learns about his environment, and fattens himself with experience. At maturity he becomes introspective. Man then develops his spiritual wings. That is why angels are characterized as having wings.

"Everything is developing from one stage to another and is in motion. Man's life is developed in seven-year cycles. Every seven years, regeneration takes place. From the age of fourteen to twenty-one is the most crucial cycle.

It will take one hundred and twenty-six years, that is, six twenty-one year cycles, to develop pure knowledge and understanding. Only then can you attain perfection. Only then are you truly wise."

It was at this point that Uncle Yah Yah paused and I noticed that the beautiful butterfly vanished from the crystal. It was replaced by the most radiant royal blue color I had ever seen. I was gazing at the blue ball when Uncle Yah Yah said, "Life is simple and can be summed up in four basic principles: Dedication, philosophy, pleasure, and the woman.

"Your way of life is whatever you are dedicated to. The most rewarding and fruitful life is in the service of, and the uplifting of, humanity. A long and active life depends on the popularity of your philosophy. The greater the need for your ideas, purpose, and aims, the greater will be the demand, and the more active your life will be. Discipline yourself to habituate healthy pleasures. Your woman is your mate, helper, and best friend. She is the precious jewel in your king's crown, and your heaven now while you live."

Distantly, I heard a knock on the door and someone saying, "Rudy, are you in there?"

Again, the knocking and the voice said, "Hey Rudy, what's up? Have you died in there?"

This time the knock was louder and so was

UNCLE YAH YAH: PART 2
21st Century Man of Wisdom

the voice. "Rudy!"

"Huh? Oh yeah. Who is it?" I called out still half asleep.

"It's me, Dottie. I brought you a breakfast tray. Open the door," she said.

"Oh, wow! Yeah, okay. Here I come. Sorry it took me so long, Dottie," I said as I hurried to open the door.

"Come on in. Put the tray down anywhere," I said as I made a quick retreat to the bathroom to wash my face and brush my teeth. I decided to shower after I ate.

"Hey Dottie," I called out, "I'm so glad you came by."

"Come on, Rudy, don't start that stuff first thing this morning," she said, interrupting me.

"What do you mean?" I asked.

"You know, about me owing you a date."

"Oh no, Dottie, this is really some serious stuff. You won't believe what happened to me last night after you and Freda left," I said excitedly. "So much happened I don't know where to start."

"Just start at the beginning," she said.

"Okay, I'll start with the UFO Report, and then I'll tell you about the dream," I said as I came out of the bathroom.

Dottie's eyes opened wide expressing

UNCLE YAH YAH: PART 2
21st Century Man of Wisdom

surprise. "The UFO what?" she asked.

"Yeah, you heard me right. It was right after you and Freda left. I was putting the manuscript away and—"

"Wait a minute, Rudy," Dottie cut in. "Before I forget, Uncle Yah Yah said he wants you to stop by the house today, first chance you get."

"Who me?" I asked.

"No, not you, Rudy. He wants to see your parakeet. Of course you," Dottie said, grinning from ear to ear.

I was silent for a moment.

"Wake up, Rudy. You were telling me about a UFO or something," she said.

"Oh yeah. Dottie you are not going to believe this. It all started when you and Freda left last night. I found an envelope with UFO Report written on it. So I opened it and . . ."

To Be Continued

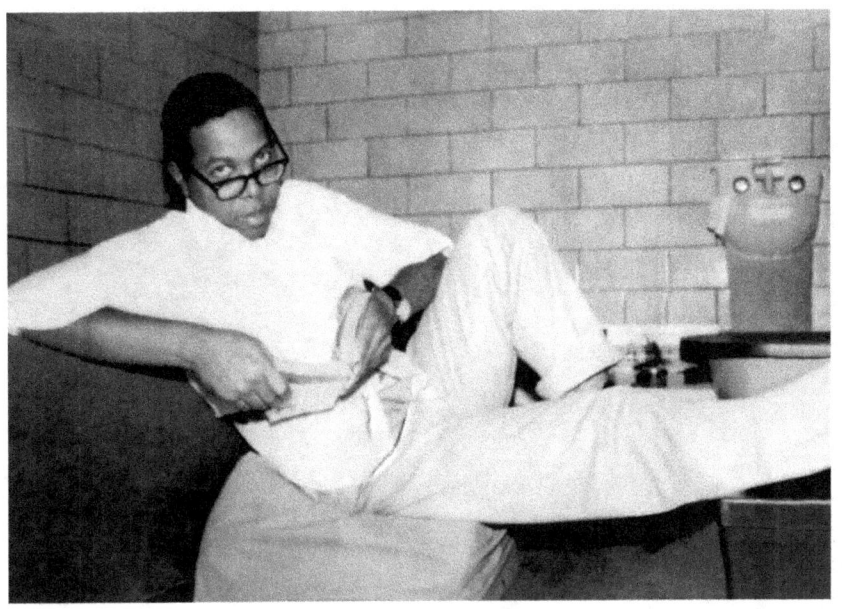

About The Author

Al Dickens was born in Winter Haven, Florida, March 31, 1938. He and his family (mother, father and sister) moved to Newark, New Jersey in the early forties. Raised in the streets of Newark's 2nd and 3rd wards made it almost inevitable that Al would start having serious trouble with the law by the age of 14. By the time he was 22 he began serving prison sentences. He was sentenced to 76 years for 18 bank robberies and two cop killings.

He served 25 years in the state penitentiary and 18 years in the federal prison system. But the prison turned out to be a golden opportunity for Al to get a formal education; and he took full advantage of it. By the time Al completed two years of college, he had co-authored three books and was working on Uncle Yah Yah. He will be released October 2010.

Yah Yah Publications
Order Form

Please Print:

Name: _____

Address: _____

City/State: _____

Zip: _____

Rush me _____ copy/copies of Uncle Yah Yah: 21st Century Man of Wisdom by Al Dickens

Price: $14.95 (US)/$18.95 Canada

Shipping/Handling: $3.95 per book $2.00 each additional book

Rush me _____ copy/copies of Uncle Yah Yah: **Part 2** by Al Dickens

Price: $19.95 (US)/$22.95 Canada

Shipping/Handling: $6.95 per book $3.00 each additional book

Total Amount enclosed $_____

Make **MONEY ORDERS & CHECKS** Payable to:
Yah Yah Publications
P.O. Box 8520 Newark, NJ 07108
Please allow 10-14 Business days for delivery

UNCLE Yah Yah

21st Century Man of Wisdom

Al Dickens

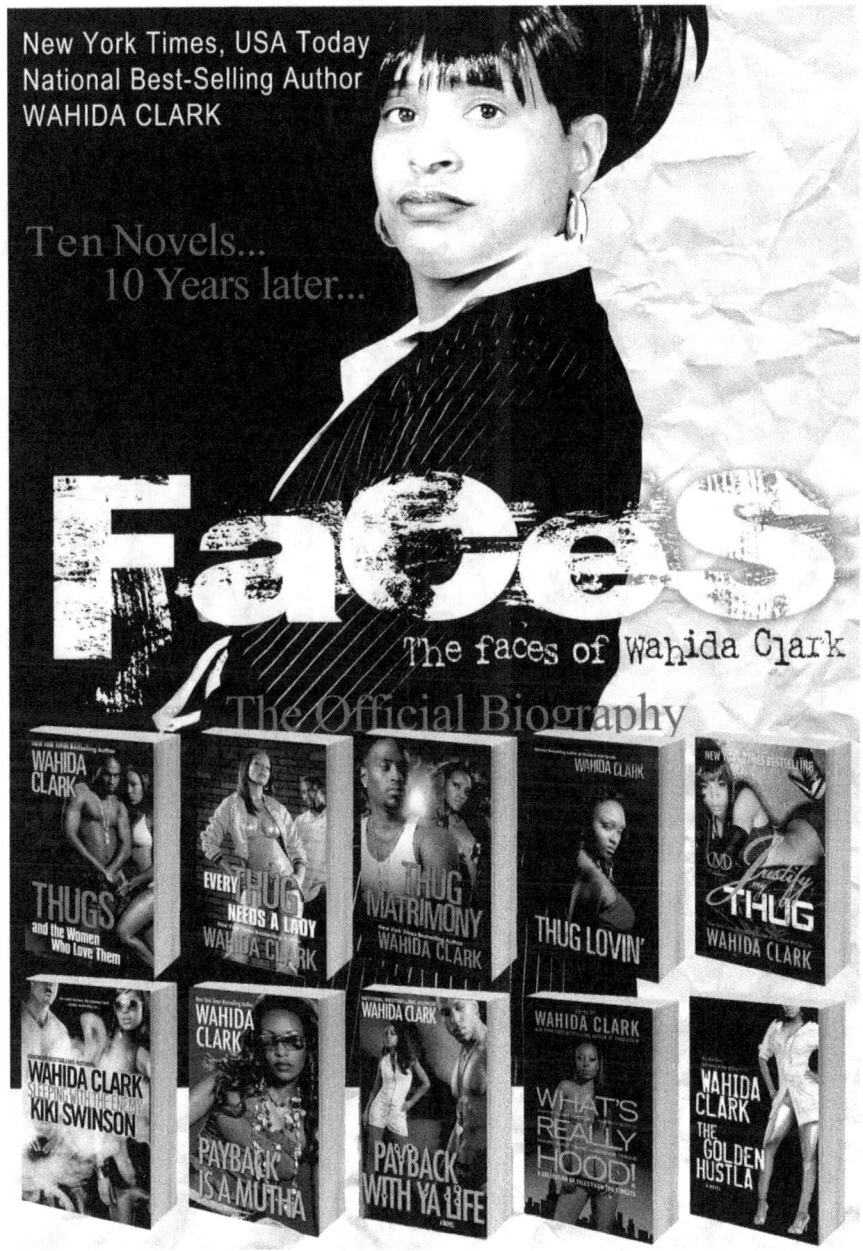